# "So...
# what are
# you
# saying?"

---

Why words are magic and
why choosing the right ones
matters now more than ever.

---

## BY DENNIS WELCH

### aBM

*"So...what are you saying?"*

Published by:
A Book's Mind
PO Box 272847
Fort Collins, CO 80527
www.abooksmind.com

ISBN 978-1-939828-98-9

# Acknowledgements

No book can be written by one person. There are always people who have made powerful contributions to the process, and this one was no exception. I may inadvertently leave someone out, but let me just try to thank those who made this book possible, either directly or indirectly.

Frankly, this would not have happened if not for my good friend Alex Charfen, and his encouragement to write this all down. Alex is a terrific encourager, and I am grateful for not only his and Cadey's friendship, but also their belief and confidence in me.

And, as you will see, I have been blessed through the years to have terrific mentors and teachers who helped me gather the knowledge I have needed to accomplish the things I have been called to do.

The Gallup Organization and its leadership gave me the opportunity to try things and to figure out what I do best. I'm eternally grateful to them.

Barbara Cave Henricks, perhaps the top book publicity mind in the business, allowed me to walk along beside her at her company for four terrific years and learn from the best.

To the many terrific authors and business people I have had the privilege of working with and representing, thank you. Just being in the room with you made me a better person.

And, to my wife Susie, and my family: thank you from the bottom of my heart for the happy life you have given me, and for a place to grow and create that is safe, and where there is unconditional love and grace.

# Contents

# Introduction

Communication used to be easier in some ways because we could focus on one medium and perhaps master it and use it to our benefit. But now, it's all coalesced into a hodgepodge of different mediums that we need to know about and master to get our point across. Put out a book and you'll need a web page (words), YouTube video (film), music (songwriting), book trailer (film and music), speech, talking points, press kit, several 500-1000 word blogs, and on and on. Every one of those things is going to have to be pitch-perfect if you plan on getting noticed.

But, precisely because of this, these are fascinating times for would-be communicators. Our influence and reach can be wider and more profound than at any time in history. Technology has allowed us to gather our "church" from around the globe and put the entire "congregation" into a single room, and we can do it in an instant.

But this new and exciting world of communication at the speed of light (or faster) has a downside. Everybody's doing it. There's a hurricane brewing. These clouds are filled with words and ideas and it's always hurricane season these days. There's a lot of noise that drowns us out and all that rumbling makes it hard to get noticed.

That's my job. To get people noticed; to help them with their messaging; to help them figure out what's important; and how to find the "hooks" that attract others to their message or idea. I love my job and I take it all very seriously, though for the most part, it is a lot of fun. I am one of those lucky guys who really does *love* coming to work every day.

And, as you'll read, I feel like I have been prepared in so many unexpected ways to do what I am doing now for my clients. I couldn't have planned all of the things that led up to this. I'm not smart enough to figure out this plan, and I definitely cannot see the future. But every step along my career and life path has been a much-needed resource that I now draw on every single day.

For example, I'm a published songwriter and I have written over 500 songs over the years. We'll talk about how songwriting helps me with all of my writing, and how having a lyrical quality to your work is important. We'll also talk about how to have an economy of words, to keep your "'song" impactful, and to save you from wandering off your message just because the words may rhyme.

But this is not a songwriting book.

I've been in the business world for a good part of my adult life. I was a senior staff writer for The Gallup Organization, and I was a director of marketing for several years. While there, I figured out how to tell our story, and start conversations that led to positive outcomes, profits, and more business.

But this is not just a marketing or business book, though the tools and stories here will hopefully help you with both.

I was also a recording artist once upon a time with an independent record deal. I was my own PR person for all those years and I had to figure out how to craft my message and make people care about me and my work.

But this is not just a PR book.

I've spent the past few years doing book publicity for some of the top authors and publishers in the country. It's been a privilege and I have learned a lot in that role.

But this is not just a book about books and publicity.

So, what kind of book is it, exactly? Well, it's a book that I hope en-courages anybody who takes the time to read it to, first of all, believe that with the right words anything is possible. It sounds a bit trite as I say that, but the stories you'll read later will tell you that it's completely true. If you can make people care about what you care about, the sky is the limit, no doubt.

And, in some ways, I've written it as a reaction to a lot of really bad communication that I get from well-meaning people who think they are doing good work. My guess is that these good people would like to communicate more effectively, but they either don't know how, or they are in too much of a hurry to pull it off.

I get those awful letters or emails or phone calls from time to time, and I can't help but think of those first few weeks of *American Idol,* where they basically make fun of those poor pitiful souls whose really awful renditions of popular songs are forever burned into our psyches. I always wonder: where are the people in your life who really care about you? Doesn't at least *one* of them know you are a terrible singer? Don't they care enough to tell you that before you embarrass yourself in front of millions of people? I always wonder what would have happened if someone had caught them early and helped them become the best singer they could be. Maybe a few tools and some training would have made all the difference for them.

And, honestly, I worry every day about being one of those delusional people who send out emails asking for meetings and action, and who is never ever being heard, or worse-they're being laughed at and derided. I don't take a lot of clients, and I get personally invested in them and their messages. Failure is not an option. So, if it takes a few extra minutes to figure out how to explain the message and messenger, and to keep that awful *American Idol* moment from happening, well, so be it.

I want my clients to win, and I want you to win. You're competing against a lot of voices out there, and much of it is at best mediocre.

And, make no mistake: It's a lot of work to get it right. But, if you do, you have a chance to sing your song, and make the difference in the world that you were intended to make.

# Drowning
## in a
# Sea of Words

One day I was sitting in the CNBC commissary in New Jersey, having coffee with my good friend and contact there. We were discussing how tough her job was as the books' contact for the station, when suddenly she offered this apology, "Hey, Dennis, if you ever don't hear from me, please don't be offended. I get 800 emails a day. I try to organize them and answer the most important ones, but sometimes I fail. So, if you don't hear from me one day, ping me again the next day, and I promise I'll answer you."

Eight hundred emails a day! Let's face it. We're all overwhelmed these days in a sea of words. Words are easier than ever to create and there is an overabundance of them, all vying for our attention. In fact, words are almost too easy to create now, in a way.

You and I spend a lot of our day and night dealing with an onslaught of instant messages, texting, and email. One study says the average teen-ager sends more than 3,000 texts a month. That's more than 100 a day! Media contacts are getting hundreds of emails every day. Your targets and friends and associates are awash in email and electronic messages of one kind or another. Oh, and just to complicate things a little more, they get old-fashioned phone calls and snail mail, too.

So, obviously, creating words is not a problem for us now. No need to chisel our messages into stone canvasses. No quills and feathers and ink wells are necessary. We don't even need cartridges and white-out to pen and erase a moment's thought or missive.

Just think about it. There was a time when writing a simple letter was a huge undertaking that required a lot of forethought and planning and attention to detail. Yes, as strange as it may seem, people used to actually write drafts of letters and put them away for a period of time so that they could go back to them and revisit what they had written to be absolutely certain that every single word was appropriate for the reader for whom it was intended.

Now words just miraculously appear under our effortless fingers and they are erased and altered with a single backstroke or by holding down the delete key. Entire thoughts can disappear with a single stroke and it's almost as if they never existed at all.

But, OMG, here's a bulletin that is as true today as it was a hundred or a thousand years ago: words matter, they can do magic, and they can make people care about what we care about—they can make us fall in love; they can soothe our aching hearts; they can make people buy our products or join our mission; they can build up a friend or tear down an enemy; and yes, they can change the world.

> OMG, here's a bulletin that is as true today as it was a hundred or a thousand years ago: words matter, they can do magic, and they can make people care about what we care about—they can make us fall in love; they can soothe our aching hearts; they can make people buy our products or join our mission; they can build up a friend or tear down an enemy; and yes, they can change the world.

That has not changed, and there is a mountain of evidence to prove it. It's delusional to think that we can fire off a quick email without taking the time to truly know our audience and assume that the impact will not matter too much one way or the other because it just so happens to be one of 500 text messages or emails we have sent this week.

It's become too easy to communicate. So easy, in fact, that we barely pay attention when we write a note or send a text. In a way, we've simultaneously devalued words at a time when they are more important than ever.

It's easy to stay busy these days, and the system is set up so that the exercise of communication feels really good. Send out some email blasts with all of the info you think people should care about and it means that you are not just sitting around waiting on something to happen. You're doing something!

I am a little bit of an introvert and so, in a way, the new technology and communication tools seem a lot more attractive. These new tools make it very easy for us introverts to stay in our space and not really have to make human contact ever. And apparently I am not the only one who's comfortable in this new world. My wife and I were in the waiting area at a local restaurant one Friday night recently, and the place was packed with people, none of whom were conversing with each other, because we were *all* checking our phones and texting without saying a single word to one other.

But, make no mistake, effective communication requires the human touch, whether we do it in person, on our phones, or in Outlook.

And yes, as hard as it is to believe, there are other very effective ways of communicating that work. For some truly successful communicators, handwritten notes, phone calls, and a visit across a desk or a table at Starbucks are all tools they are using to change the world a little. Doug Conant, former CEO of Campbell's Soup, built one of the world's most engaged workforces by doing three simple but very consistent things: he put on a pedometer and walked the Campbell's complex in Camden, New Jersey, every day and had simple but powerful conversations with all of the people there, and listened to their needs and ideas and then followed through on them. Doug also sent out over 30,000 handwritten notecards over a decade as CEO. I have one in my office that he sent me during the publicity campaign we did on his best-selling book *Touchpoints* that he co-authored with his friend Mette Norgaard.

## When It's Really, Really Important...

Fed Ex has an ad that says: "When it's really, really important that it get there overnight...." And it closes with an admonition to call the good people at Fed Ex and they will deliver it every day right on time. If only it was that easy to deliver our important messages that we send out every day. It's tough to get through to people these days, and there are a lot of reasons.

First and foremost, we have too many competing messages and throngs of messengers, and because of that, we are distracted. New research says that the average knowledge worker in this country is interrupted about

> The right words, carefully chosen and pieced together—in whatever form they take—are as mysterious as they ever were. They're powerful, and they still move people and they still get things done.

every 12 minutes. And, because it's a whole 12 minutes between interruptions, we interrupt ourselves every 3-4 minutes to check voice mail and email and our phones for possible texts, etc. It's a cluttered world, with lots of noise and all of it seems urgent and it calls to us even when we want to shut it off.

Small wonder that so many of us are being diagnosed with ADD. It's actually a marvel to me that we don't all have at least a touch of it. We're overwhelmed every day with so many stimuli that it's really amazing that we ever get anything done.

But, I'm here to give you some encouraging news. You *can* get your message through and you *can* make people care about your product or idea or philosophy.

You can.

It's not easy, but there are people doing it every day, even in this cluttered environment with the onslaught of verbiage and texts and IMs, etc.

Why? Because the right words, carefully chosen and pieced together—in whatever form they take—are as mysterious as they ever were. They're powerful, and they still move people and they still get things done.

# Why Me?

I've always been in love with words and in some ways that love affair began at a very young age, and even then it was inexplicable and mysterious. I could read and write before I ever started school, and I discovered that I had this talent quite by accident. My mother came home one fine December evening and told my father that she had been to see S-A-N-T-A C-L-A-U-S. I said (much to her and my dad's great surprise), "You've been to see Santa Claus?"

It got really quiet for just a split second, and then my mother asked if I knew what she had just spelled, or if perhaps I had discovered it some other way or from some other source (perhaps my sneaky brother). In my mind it was no big deal. Why were we even discussing it? Of course, I could spell Santa Claus, and it didn't seem like much of a miracle at the time. I guess that I had somehow taught myself to spell with a crude version of phonics, and emulation and outright curiosity. Mom told some of our more formally educated relatives about the "Santa Claus episode," and soon one of them would take me out to the University of Houston to be tested. I sort of remember that, the foreign-ness of it all.

I must have done well on the tests, because when I started school at Janowski Elementary in inner-city Houston, they wanted to put me in in the third grade. My mother wisely said a resounding NO to that idea, and they started me in the first grade with all the other 6 years olds.

On day one of the first grade, our school Principal, Mrs. McRee, an austere, no-nonsense woman with dark-rimmed glasses, walked into Mrs. Elzy's class and asked me to step out into the hallway with her for a moment. My class was just beginning a reading circle, ostensibly a time every day for us to read out of a book of some kind and, I surmised with my 6-year old intuition, learn how to spell *Santa Claus* for ourselves.

Mrs. McRee—to whom, by the way, I am eternally grateful—took me out of class that first day of school and walked me down to the school library. I remember that huge metal library door creaking a little as it swung open, and before long we were standing in the midst of a wonderland of books and the inky smell of mostly hardback tomes neatly arranged in colorful rows in what I assumed at the time must have been the biggest library in the whole wide world. She escorted me straight to the far side of the room, the side with windows that looked out on to Bauman Road, the street that ran directly in front of the school. Mrs. McRee—we first-grade boys would later, in jest, call her "Old Iron Pants" as the years went on there—gracefully raised her arm and motioned to the shelf directly in front of us. Remember, it was my first day of school, she was *the principal*, and she had my undivided attention.

"Dennis, these are the books for children in grades 1, 2, and 3," she said very authoritatively and with no obvious emotion. "*The Cat in the Hat, Horton Hears a Who...* that kind of thing."

Then we walked to our left and stood near the southwest corner with the windows at our back, and looked out from that hallowed ground to the rest of the library with what I was sure must have been a million books.

"The rest of this library is filled with books for the big boys and girls, grades 4, 5, and 6. You may come down here, Dennis, during the reading circle time every day and you can have the run of the place and pick out any book from anywhere you want."

"Every day?" I asked.

"Every day."

"Any book?"

"Any book."

My heart leapt as I walked around the place, slowly perusing the shelves and running my finger over the spine of *Charlotte's Web, Thirty Seconds Over Tokyo, The Mickey Mantle Story,* and the complete collection of Mark Twain. I read all of those books before I left Janowski School, some several times. It left such an indelible impression on me that even after almost 50 years, provided that they haven't moved anything, I could still walk into that room and show you exactly where the green hardback version of *Charlotte's Web* was on the shelf, and do the same for the red-and-white hardcover version of *The Mickey Mantle Story,* and on and on.

Recently, I read *Charlotte's Web* for the first time in probably 45 or 50 years. It was interesting how quickly it all came back, the sadness at Charlotte's passing; the appreciation for her sacrifice on Wilbur's behalf. I realized as I read that my reaction to words has always been different. I've never just read words on the page in a clinical way. Somehow the words get down into my soul and they change me and affect me to my core. That innate and mysterious ability has served me well through the years in the various roles I've played. Because of it, I can really sense how words will be perceived and understood on the other end by the listener.

Mrs. McRee couldn't have known at the time the impact this simple gesture would have on my life and the lives of those I've had the privilege of working with through the years.

I'm certain that she has gone on to her great reward by now, but every time I read a good book, or write something that moves me or someone else, I give a little wink and a nod toward the southwest corner of Janowski School, and hope that wherever "Old Iron Pants" is, she knows how grateful I am.

## Nothing is Wasted

One of the questions I ask in my bio interviews is: "When did you know you had these very specific and amazing gifts?" My answer to that question is that I always sort of knew I had them, but I really started figuring it out after I became a singer and songwriter and had to do my own PR.

I grew up in a home where music was not particularly revered, and no one sang or played an instrument. Then, out of the blue, my oldest brother Michael started playing guitar and my older brother Keith started singing at gospel music gatherings in the Houston area. My brothers were both quite good, and while I envied them from afar, I never intended to take up music or play an instrument or sing anywhere except in church on Sundays and Wednesdays.

One night, while driving home from a date, the strangest thing happened. I started singing and writing a song about Heaven, completely out of the thin air and with no notice of any kind. I didn't have a radio in my yellow 1972 VW bug, and it was a long drive home. One by one, lines of the song kept appearing to me that night in my mind's eye, and I would dutifully add the new line to the song and keep singing.

In fact, I kept singing the song over and over again on my drive home so I could remember it, and when I got home, I quickly wrote it down. The next day, I went to my job at Sleep-N-Aire Mattress Company and I couldn't stop thinking about the song that I had just written the night before. My good friend Mike Simpson was also my boss, and played guitar; he and his wife sang in my church every week. They were amazing singers and multi-talented people, and I really admired them, though I never actually planned to follow in their footsteps, either.

I didn't want to admit to Mike that day that I had written a song because I was actually afraid he might make fun of me or crack a joke about it. So, I stood near his desk while he worked and I sort of hummed it and sang parts of it as if it was something I had just heard on the radio. Eventually after a few verses, he asked me what song I was singing. Only then did I reluctantly admit to him that it was something I had written only the night before.

Mike always had his Ovation guitar at the office, so he opened the case, took it out, and figured out the chords I was singing. Then, he started playing it while we both sang it. It was so amazing to hear him sing it and play it on his guitar. It was a wonderful and completely unforgettable moment, the opposite of what I thought would happen. In fact, that single moment would inspire me to write again and again. Over the years, I have written over 500 songs. And, every time I do, I am thankful for that early encouragement. In a way, my friend Mike has a part in every song I've ever written. When I see him on occasion, I remind him of that.

After he and I sang a few rounds of the song that day in his little office, Mike suggested that I get a guitar and learn some chords for myself. So, I went out and bought a 100 dollar Ventura guitar, thinking that if I wound up not liking it or not being able to play it, I could just sell it or give it away. Little did I know that those hundred bucks would probably be some of the best money I would ever spend. I did learn some new chords, but I had a really good and completely unexpected problem—I couldn't learn new chords without hearing words to go along with them. In those first days of learning to play guitar, I wrote dozens of songs and I thought I was becoming a really good songwriter because things rhymed and they sort of sounded like what I heard on the radio.

(Let me just pause and say that if you are thinking, "Wait a minute, I'm not a songwriter, so why should I care about this part of the story?' I would answer that there are a lot of lessons about creativity and communication here and, frankly, these apply to everything I have ever done since then. Think about it: a songwriter has about three minutes to make his or her point, to make us care enough to listen again, and maybe even buy their product. It's sort of the ultimate in targeted messaging, isn't it?)

One day, a few years later, when I thought I had really arrived as a songwriter, I met a man named Kemper Crabb. We became very good friends, and he was a mentor for me in a lot of ways. His wife gave me voice lessons and I was a frequent visitor to their house. Kemper fronted a very successful band at the time called Ark Angel, and he was and is a gifted songwriter. One night he came out to a gig I was doing, and afterward he took me aside and challenged me.

13

> Want to be a great communicator? Get quiet, turn off your radio, take long drives, sit in silence. Think about your audience. Listen. Find a co-writer, a Challenger in Chief who will help you improve and who will NOT pull punches when asked to review your work.

He said, "I know you think you're a good songwriter, but quite frankly you settle too often for words that rhyme so you can get the songs done and move on to the next one. In a way, you are obligated to be so much better than that. Let me show you what some of the truly great songwriters are doing with words."

The next night, I drove out to his little apartment in Pasadena, Texas, and took my weekly voice lesson. When I left to go back home that evening, he sent me home with three albums: *Netherlands* and *Souvenirs,* by Dan Fogelberg, and a Leonard Cohen record. I drove back home, and later that night I dropped the needle down on the *Netherlands* album. From the opening line, I was both stunned by the beauty of it and humbled by its greatness.

I made it through the *Netherlands* album, and by the time I finally listened to the title track on *Souvenirs,* I was a basket case. I wanted to put my pencil and guitar away and never try again. Or—even better—I wanted to pick it all back up and do something different, something better, something more complete. I'll never forget the feeling that came over me when Dan Fogelberg sang so beautifully about a man sifting through a drawer of memories and then pausing to sing the chorus:

*Down in the Canyon, the smoke starts to rise*

*It rides on the wind until it reaches your eyes*

*When faced with the past, the strongest man cries.*

When faced with this kind of writing, I suddenly felt inadequate and weak, like a slacker who had settled for just any words and not THE words that would tell the stories I cared about. It made me angry at first to be pushed like that by Kemper and told that I was not doing my best work. But one listen to one song on any of those albums told me that he was right, and God bless him for his honesty and for caring enough to challenge me to get better.

Want to be a great communicator? Get quiet, turn off your radio, take long drives, sit in silence. Think about your audience. Listen. Find a co-writer, a Challenger in Chief who will help you improve and who will NOT pull punches when asked to review your work.

Your song will surely come wafting in one night on the evening breeze. Write it down and re-write it. Then, visualize someone listening to your song when you send it over, and write it again. Find people who will challenge you to write your best song, the anthem for your product, idea, book, or company.

Then you will be amazed at what happens when you sing it. I was.

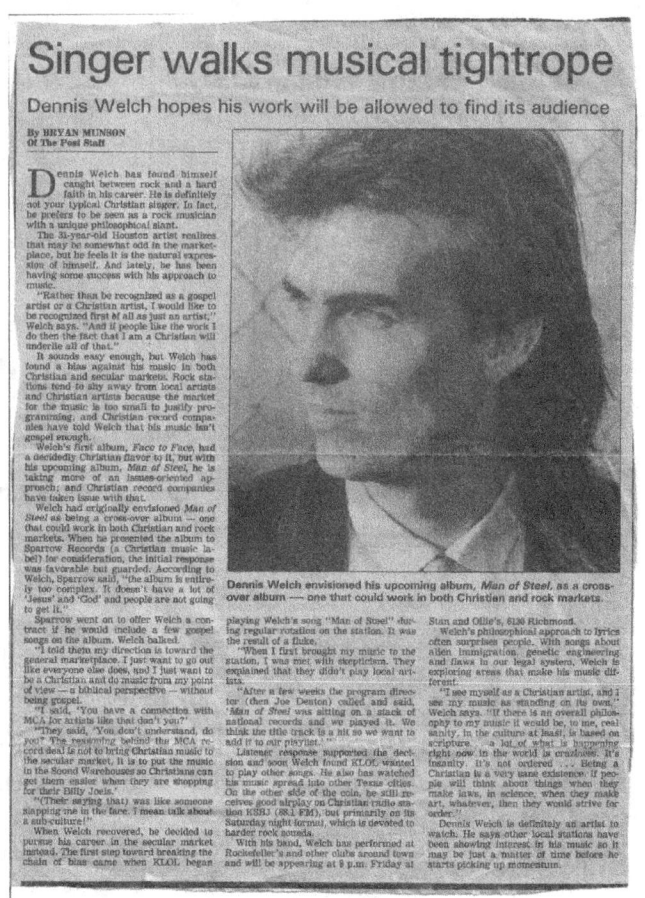

**Singer walks musical tightrope**

Dennis Welch hopes his work will be allowed to find its audience

By BRYAN MUNSON
Of The Post Staff

Dennis Welch has found himself caught between rock and a hard faith in his career. He is definitely not your typical Christian singer. In fact, he prefers to be seen as a rock musician with a unique philosophical slant.

The 31-year-old Houston artist realizes that may be somewhat odd in the marketplace, but he feels it is the natural expression of himself. And lately, he has been having some success with his approach to music.

"Rather than be recognized as a gospel artist or a Christian artist, I would like to be recognized first of all as just an artist," Welch says. "And if people like the work I do then the fact that I am a Christian will underlie all of that."

It sounds easy enough, but Welch has found a bias against his music in both Christian and secular markets. Rock stations tend to shy away from local artists and Christian artists because the market for the music is too small to justify programming, and Christian record companies have told Welch that his music isn't gospel enough.

Welch's first album, Face to Face, had a decidedly Christian flavor to it, but with his upcoming album, Man of Steel, he is taking more of an issues-oriented approach; and Christian record companies have taken issue with that.

Welch had originally envisioned Man of Steel as being a cross-over album — one that could work in both Christian and rock markets. When he presented the album to Sparrow Records (a Christian music label) for consideration, the initial response was favorable but guarded. According to Welch, Sparrow said, "the album is entirely too complex. It doesn't have a lot of 'Jesus' and 'God' and people are not going to get it."

Sparrow went on to offer Welch a contract if he would include a few gospel songs on the album. Welch balked.

"I told them my direction is toward the general marketplace. I just want to go out like everyone else does, and I just want to be a Christian and do music from my point of view — a biblical perspective — without being gospel.

"I said, 'You have a connection with MCA for artists like that don't you?'

"They said, 'You don't understand, do you? The reasoning behind the MCA record deal is not to bring Christian music to the secular market. It is to put the music in the Sound Warehouses so Christians can get them easier when they are shopping for their Billy Joels.'

"(Their saying that) was like someone slapping me in the face. I mean talk about a sub-culture!"

When Welch recovered, he decided to pursue his career in the secular market instead. The first step toward breaking the chain of bias came when KLOL began playing Welch's song "Man of Steel" during regular rotation on the station. It was the result of a fluke.

"When I first brought my music to the station, I was met with skepticism. They explained that they didn't play local artists.

"After a few weeks the program director (then Joe Denton) called and said, 'Man of Steel was sitting on a stack of national records and we played it. We think the the track is a bit so we want to add it to our playlist.'"

Listener response supported the decision and soon Welch found KLOL wanted to play other songs. He also has watched his music spread into other Texas cities. On the other side of the coin, he still receives good airplay on Christian radio station KSBJ (88.1 FM), but primarily on its Saturday night format, which is devoted to harder rock sounds.

With his band, Welch has performed at Rockefeller's and other clubs around town and will be appearing at 9 p.m. Friday at Stan and Ollie's, 6130 Richmond.

Welch's philosophical approach to lyrics often surprises people. With songs about alien immigration, genetic engineering and flaws in our legal system, Welch is exploring areas that make his music different.

"I see myself as a Christian artist, and I use my music as standing on its own," Welch says. "If there is an overall philosophy to my music it would be, to me, really sanity. In the culture at least, is based on scripture. ... a lot of what is happening right now in the world is craziness. It's insanity. It's not ordered ... Being a Christian is a very sane existence. If people will think about things when they make laws, in science, when they make art, whatever, then they would strive for order."

Dennis Welch is definitely an artist to watch. He says other local stations have been showing interest in his music so it may be just a matter of time before he starts picking up momentum.

Dennis Welch envisioned his upcoming album, Man of Steel, as a cross-over album — one that could work in both Christian and rock markets.

15

## Early Days of PR by the Bootstraps

One day, I realized that I had written enough good songs to record a long playing album, an LP of my material. Through some miraculous twists and turns, I found myself in a world-class recording studio with some of the best session players in the world and a remarkable engineer. The producer was Kemper Crabb, my friend who had cared enough to challenge me to do better work and to take my time to craft the message of each song into the best it could be. He was intent on producing the recording and he did and amazing job. Paul Mills was the engineer, and he arranged all of the orchestration on the songs as well. Paul was and is a genius, in my opinion. We use that word too often, but in Paul's case, I say it is true.

Let me just interject something here that is probably becoming obvious to you: I have always been blessed by having just the right people who show up at just the right time with exactly what I need to hear or learn. It's uncanny, really, how often it has happened in my life, and you'll see that thread throughout these stories. I feel very humbled by that. It's another mystery that I do not understand completely, but am eternally thankful for.

The record, *Face to Face*, turned out to be an independently released record (in the book industry, we would call it self-published) and I was in charge of doing all the marketing and PR if anyone was ever to hear about it, and if it was going to make any kind of small difference in the world. Even at that early age (I was in my mid- twenties) I figured out that I had to decide what was important and be able to get to that in a hurry. It was my elevator speech, though I don't think anyone was actually calling it that at the time.

Keep in mind that there were no cell phones, no email, no technology besides the old-fashioned phone and snail mail. I sat down and wrote out a script that I decided to use on every call to every radio and TV station around Houston and in other parts of Texas. I decided that these were the differentiators: Kemper Crabb had produced it, and quite a few people knew him and knew his name. Even better: the studio band was Andrae Crouch's touring band. Andrae was perhaps the most famous black gospel singer of the day, and his band was world class. And, finally, the studio—Rivendell—was the home of a lot of great contemporary Christian hit songs of the day, and a lot of people sort of knew that, even though Contemporary Christian Music (CCM) was still in its relative infancy. I somehow figured that having all these elements gave me credibility and gave it to me quickly, without having to explain things in great detail to a stranger on the other end of the line who was tapping their toe while they figured out how long the conversation was or was not going to last. I hoped that these elements would get their attention quickly and hold it.

Thankfully, my "script" worked beautifully, and soon I found myself going all over Texas and Louisiana doing TV shows and radio interviews. Radio stations played my music in rapid rotation and we got a chance to open for some of the bigger stars of the day. Though I didn't know it at the time, that was great practice for what I do now, and I got very good at it.

## All Publicity is Good Publicity (Well, most of the time)

One day, during this flurry of promotional activity, I learned a really important lesson. I was a guest on an Austin, Texas TV show called *Eleven With Barbara Miller*. I was the only guest for the entire hour and, I have to say, for the first fifty minutes or so it was going along swimmingly. I sang a few songs, we talked about the album, the recording, and writing process, and I was pleased. The host seemed pleased, too. We had a good conversation going on, and it was almost over, or so I thought.

But then, right near the end of it all, she asked a perfectly legitimate question that I was wholly unprepared for.

Oops.

"So Dennis, what do you think of Contemporary Christian Music?"

And what I said next was, well, not well-thought-out to say the least, and it came off slightly arrogant and proved to be excellent fodder for being totally misunderstood.

"I think most of what we as Christians produce as art these days is derivative and not terribly original. In CCM, we have the *Christian Kenny Loggins* and all of that, but we shouldn't be doing that. Bach wasn't the Christian Beethoven, he was Johann Sebastian Bach for Heaven's sakes! Totally original and better than everyone. We should be like that instead of picking people in the secular music arena, mimicking their already terrific work, and turning it into Jesus music."

That sound you hear now is the sound of what was the beginning of a fairly promising career going down the drain. Ms. Miller was gracious enough and somehow we muddled through that moment and finished the show.

When the hour (was it only an hour?) was officially over, an obviously perturbed producer walked over to me and said, "Well, big boy, you need to come with me." We marched over to a bank of phones, all lit up and white-hot with unhappy fans of Contemporary Christian Music, and he said, "You see all those blinking lines (I think the word he used was 'blinking')? Well, those are all for *you*, and you're going to answer *every single* (I think the word he used was 'single') one of them!"

And I did. I picked up the first blinking line and wow… I got an earful asking me in a very shrill and angry voice just who I thought I was, criticizing… And on and on it went, every line and every shrill voice all saying basically the same thing. It was disheartening, to say the least. It was live TV and there was no chance to take it back. I was unprepared, though I did say what I was thinking and really believed. But, admittedly, I could have found a better way to say it.

I walked out of the TV studio and got into my car with what was left of my posterior, and thought, well, it's been a nice run. I did one record, I had a few minutes in the sun, but now, I need to get back to selling furniture and figure out what I'm going to do next with my life.

Thankfully another lesson or two was in store; one that I have most certainly never forgotten. I didn't have a record distributor, so I had come to Austin the day before and stocked all the shelves (on consignment) at all of the Christian bookstores and music sellers. After I got through answering all the calls I pulled over and called Kemper and told him what had happened on the show.

He said, "Wait. Before you kill yourself, why don't you drive around to some of the stores and see if you sold any records?"

One by one I drove around to all of them and guess what? They had all sold out of Dennis Welch *Face to Face* records!

All of them.

The lessons here? Well there are a lot of lessons, but here are the most important ones:

Always prepare for interviews, and always plan as best you can for unexpected questions. By the way, this lesson is not just for people who'll be appearing on TV or radio. It's for all of us. Every day. In every moment. Be prepared.

> Always prepare for interviews, and always plan as best you can for unexpected questions. By the way, this lesson is not just for people who'll be appearing on TV or radio. It's for all of us. Every day. In every moment. Be prepared.

The second lesson? All publicity is for the most part, good publicity, and like the old Hollywood adage says, just be sure they spell your name right.

The third lesson? Sometimes, no matter how much you prepare, you're going to blow it anyway. Don't despair. Resolve to do better next time, then take a drive around and see if you've sold all your LPs, figuratively speaking. Remember, everybody fails and if you don't try at all, your chances of winning are zero. It takes a lot of guts to be on live TV or radio and feel the heat of the moment. It takes intestinal fortitude to pick up the phone for a sales call, knowing you'll likely be met with hostility or, at best, indifference. You will make mistakes occasionally. But, prepare like crazy, and remind yourself often that that you're there, you're in the game, and the potential for greatness and for making a difference rises exponentially because you made the effort and showed up.

## Just a Word or Two about Presentation

You'll note that in the previous section I did not ever show the actual album cover for my first record, *Face to Face*. The kindest thing I can say about it is that it was not very good, but it was all a part of the learning process, and at the time I knew absolutely nothing about presentation and the impact that can have on the outcomes you are seeking. I spent a lot of money and time making this really wonderful debut recording and I spent zero time on the cover art for it. And, that faux pas was obvious to everyone except me. And, even though some terrific things happened on the publicity front for that album, it probably could have been even better if I had taken a little more time and put all the hard work we put into making a good recording into a representative package.

So, when I got ready to make my second album, I decided that I would find the best album art director that I could afford, and it turned out to be one of the best decisions I had made about my career up to that time. Joan Tankersley was busy building a remarkable reputation as an album art director, was winning awards for her work, and selling quite a few records for her clients in the process.

We sat down one day in a restaurant over coffee and I asked her if she would be willing to do the art for my new record that we had just finished, *Man of Steel*. It was a 6-song Rock EP, and the title track was one of the strongest songs I had ever written up to that time. She agreed to take me on as a client, and then what happened next is one of those moments that I'll never forget, mainly because I didn't understand a single word of the "conversation" we had about what she thought the album art should be. I remember her saying something about a giant metal object in the background, blue goggles, a red rose, a tux coat, grease, and…after a few paragraphs of her trying to explain to me what turned out to be an amazing concept, she saw that my eyes had glazed over and that I was not following her at all.

Finally, she said, "Look, just show up at the studio on Tuesday and we'll get to work. Trust me."

So, Tuesday morning, I dutifully showed up at the studio and it was quite a day for a guy who doesn't see pictures at all. You can describe something all day to me in conceptual form, but I don't really grasp it until I see it. Indeed, just as Joan had predicted, there was a large metal object as a backdrop, and yes there were blue goggles, a welder's mitt made out of chain, and a tux coat. Lots of grease.

But here is the outcome:

As you can guess, there were a lot of positives from taking the time to get it right this time. Let me just talk about one for a minute. At the time, no local band or artist had received rapid rotation airplay on a Houston rock station since ZZ Top, way back when. Undaunted, I drove down to KLOL radio on Lovett Street and walked in to find a fairly surly receptionist who, not surprisingly, gave me a surly reception commensurate with her position and talent. She was obviously hired because she matched the *Go Away* motif of the reception area.

"May I help you?" she said, with all the condescension she could muster.

I explained that I was a local artist, I had just finished this recording, and I would like to drop it off for the program director to consider for airplay.

She laughed out loud as she took it from me, holding it slightly away from her as if it had some kind of communicative disease. I was surprised that she didn't use tongs and gloves to keep from being infected.

"We don't play local artists."

(Awkward silence.)

And then, I said:

"Well, why don't you just keep it anyway? If you don't like the record, you can always heat it up in your oven and make a nice ash tray."

Considerably less awkward silence—even a little laughter from Attila the Hun-ess at my lame attempt at a joke. Another important lesson: It's amazing what a little humor can do to break seemingly unbreakable ice.

And, I thanked her for her time and walked away, thinking that *Man of Steel* was probably already in the oven, figuratively speaking.

## A Breakthrough

But then a miracle of sorts happened. On a particularly cold and dreary October afternoon, my phone rang and a strange voice I had never heard before was on the other end of the line.

"Dennis, this is Denton Marr, program director at KLOL radio. You got a minute?"

He went on to tell me that as a rule they did not play any local artists, and that 100 percent of their airplay list came from national labels, and suggested singles always came from promotion men hired by the labels or the artists themselves. But he was about to make a very large and very, very rare exception.

"Somehow, your record, *Man of Steel*, wound up in a stack of national records that we were listening to and considering for airplay. *Man of Steel* looked like a national record, so we assumed that it was. When we dropped the needle down on the title track, we were stunned. *Man of Steel* is a great song, and we think it has potential. We'd like to add it to our daily airplay rotation if you're ok with that. Can you bring me a couple more copies of the record?"

For a recording artist, this was a conversation that you dream about. Even better, for the next few months, I drove around Houston and heard my song five times a day coming on after Phil Collins, Blue Oyster Cult, or Journey.

> Pay attention to ALL the details. Write great messages. Then, couch them in the best vehicle possible. Know what you don't know and hire experts to fill in the gaps. If you do, you're giving your "song" the best chance to be heard by the most people. And when that happens, literally anything is possible.

Pretty amazing, and I would say that the presentation had almost everything to do with that outcome. The program director thought it was a national record before he ever heard the first note.

And, I understand that other rock stations around Texas played the song as well after KLOL started playing it. We sold quite a few records in the stores, and we heard that people would walk into the store, see the album on display, and ask someone to play it out of sheer curiosity.

The lessons here? Pay attention to ALL the details. Write great messages. Then, couch them in the best vehicle possible. Know what you don't know and hire experts to fill in the gaps.

If you do, you're giving your "song" the best chance to be heard by the most people. And when that happens, literally anything is possible.

## Sometimes You are Right Where You're Supposed to Be

I've been blessed, and I know it. I have been on a remarkable adventure for most of my life, and the vehicle that has taken me there has always been forged from one form of words or another. In my early days, it was music and lyrics. I had some success, and then one day, I just couldn't do the performing part anymore. I had recorded a Rock and Roll record that was getting airplay around the country, I had signed an independent record deal, and I was out on the road getting to see the touring life firsthand. Our kids were very young, and every night at the end of each show, I would call home and they would ask me again and again when I was going to be coming back to Texas. And when I had to tell them night after night that I didn't know when I'd be coming home, it broke me down and tore my heart in two. I stayed out on this little tour for three whole weeks and honestly it seemed like three years. I started in Minneapolis, and by the time I got to Salt Lake City 21 days later, I was a mess. I was sad, I hated music, and I couldn't imagine doing it for a living as a performer; ever.

Someone once said that we oftentimes climb the ladder of success only to find that it was against the wrong wall. I was the poster boy for that adage, and it was time for me to face up to it and go home and figure out what I was going to do next. When our musical circus rolled into Salt Lake early on the morning of that 21st day, I didn't even go to sleep. I went straight to a phone and called the manager who had sent me out there in the first place, and I told him I couldn't go on. To my surprise, he said he had already figured that out, and he understood completely. He was kind and gracious. He told me to go out to the airport, and that he'd have a ticket back home waiting for me. And, he kept his word.

The next day, I flew home from Utah wondering what in the world I was going to do next. I had worked as a telephone interviewer for The Tarrance Group, a conservative polling outfit, before I had gone out on this little three-week trek. When I came home, I called them and asked if I could go back to work in their phone room doing political surveys and market research. They gladly took me back, and I went back to work, but they let me know that there would be changes. They told me they were being sold to The Gallup Organization and that the transition could happen almost anytime over the next few weeks. I couldn't have known it at the time, but this was about to be another life-altering moment that literally changed the trajectory of my life forever.

And, just as an aside, let me say this: Even doing phone surveys night after night was a terrific lesson in writing a great script. Just think about it—people around the country were sitting down in the evening to have dinner with their families and here we were calling and disturbing them to ask about imported beer and who should be governor. That survey had better be good and concise, and it had better hold their attention for the entire 10-15 minutes (or more) that we were on the phone together. The good ones were just that—good. But when the Tarrance Group became the Gallup Organization, there was an obvious and gigantic leap forward in the writing quality and style of these instruments. Shortly after the transition, I remember doing a Gallup Youth Survey that was written by George Gallup, Jr., and it was an absolute thing of beauty. We were talking to kids age 13 to 18, and getting them to do the survey in the first place was going to be a challenge. As I recall, we had to get their parents' permission first (an extra hurdle), and then we would do an 18-20 minute survey that covered the gamut of issues they faced as teenagers growing up in America. The survey itself would start out kind of shallow with questions about fairly light subjects, and then would proceed to gradually get deeper into all kinds of issues—politics, religion, and current events. Often, I would ask the last question in the survey, and, to my surprise, those kids would ask with some sadness in their voice, "Are we really done? You don't have any more questions for me?" They loved that we were asking their opinions. For some, it may have been the very first time.

I later became great friends with George Gallup, Jr. and his wife Kingsley, and they wrote the forward for my memoir, *Rich People Shop Here*. I realized as I got to know him that along with being one of the kindest and gentlest people I have ever known, he was something of a genius. The ability to write great questions was obviously passed down in the DNA from his famous and groundbreaking father, George Sr., on down to George, Jr.

and his brother Alec. The timing and cadence of each question he wrote was impeccable and time flew by. Not a single word was wasted, and it was like reading a great piece of literature on the phone, a bedtime story penned by a great author instead of a stodgy old telephone survey that no one wants to do in the first place.

Anyway, I immediately recognized it for what it was: a lyrical thing of beauty, almost musical. George and the Gallup team had a gift, and all one had to do to see the difference was to just try any other phone survey and attempt to keep people on the phone for any length of time, much less kids who had the focus of a gnat. And yet, night after night I saw it happen over and over again. I lived it, and once again I stood amazed at the power of just the right words in just the right order to compel people to stay and answer and care.

Just like a great song or a great book, George's words evoked strong emotions and deep thought. I remember that one of those surveys got all the way down to the last questions, and then, it posed pointed and poignant ones about Jesus. "Do you believe He was just a good man, or was He the Son of God, or…"

Fascinating. I thought kids would get tired and hang up or just mentally check out. But no. They not only did *not* check out, they were moved. *By a telephone survey*, of all things! And night after night, they let me know that they were even a little disappointed when we ran out of questions to ask. I miss George, and the world misses his work and his ability to get the information out of us to help make the world a better place. I'm not sure who has replaced him at The Gallup Organization, but those are some mighty big shoes to fill.

# Magic Stories

# Preaching "The Gospel" at Gallup

When I finished MBA school in 1998, I was still working for The Gallup Organization. I had done several things at Gallup, including running a telephone interviewing center and starting Spanish interviewing from the ground up. Yes, there was a time at The Gallup Organization where if we called you and you answered "Hola," we didn't talk with you because we couldn't. I and an amazing and sometimes superhuman team of Spanish interviewers, translators, and the greatest recruiter I have ever known came together to make this happen. It was a remarkable time, really, and in my last year in the role of Director of Hispanic Interviewing, we conducted almost 120,000 interviews in Spanish or Portuguese.

But after graduating from MBA school, I wanted to try my hand at marketing. Gallup was beginning to transform itself from a very well-known but not terribly profitable polling company into a consulting force to be reckoned with, but the marketing we used had not changed much. So, on the first day on my new job as a director of marketing for our Dallas office, I got my marching orders from my new boss.

"You'll make a hundred phone calls a day, every day," he said.

I already hated the job and I had only had it for ten seconds. But, it got worse.

"And, you'll have two conversations a day. That's ten conversations a week, and we have all the data to say that for every ten conversations you'll set up one meeting…."

I was already glazing over and looking around for the bottle of poison pills.

Here's what I was really thinking while he was talking: REALLY? This is how we do marketing for the NEW Gallup, the NEW consulting juggernaut we are building? Something was wrong with this picture and here's what I saw as the problem. Polling was all about price and there was often no long-lasting relationship or trust. People needed data; we provided data; we get paid. If we charge more than the guy down the street we don't get the gig. No discussion. All these opportunities for polling were refereed by a troll who lived in the basement of most big companies. He was never allowed to see the light of day, the dirge music played every day when he entered the building, and he had no vision and certainly no need for an actual relationship or a level of trust.

As I understood it, that was *not* what we were doing now, or at least hoping to do. We were becoming in a way, personal trainers, and you just *have* to trust your personal trainer, yes? And that sure as heck is *not* going to happen in a two-minute phone call where you have been dragged out of a meeting by a guy making a hundred phone calls a day.

## Visitation

I was certain that there *must* be a better way to build the kind of relationships and trust that were required to get inside of a company and live with it and become its "personal trainer." I called our CEO and offered this alternate idea to the 100 phone call plan—why not set up an email box called "New Discoveries@ Gallup.com" and just invite people to join us and learn from us? After all, we had 70-plus years of data to draw from, had seen everything, and had some of the smartest people on the planet. What business leader in his or her right mind wouldn't want to learn what we had learned?

I made this analogy to our CEO when I pitched the New Discoveries idea. He asked where the seeds of this idea were sown and I told him that I grew up in the Baptist church, and on Tuesday nights every week, we had something called visitation, a time where we went out into the community, door-to-door, to invite people to come to church on Sunday. I was always fascinated by the range of responses we would get on those Tuesday nights. Sometimes people would open the door and ask what time church started on Sunday, and sure enough Sunday morning would come around and they'd be there just as promised. Sometimes people were ugly and slammed the door in our faces. And, there were all kinds of responses that fell somewhere between anger and attendance. Why? Why the extremely wide spectrum of responses? I contend that it had less to do with us being there and knocking on their door, and almost everything to do with what happened before we got there. People were busy living with their situations, learning from them, gathering information to help them solve their problem, and analyzing it all every day.

And, I was gambling that the same is true of effective marketing communications. Companies are living with their situation, they are unsure of what to do next to solve their problems, they face pressure to solve the issues or lose their jobs, and they are open to new ideas and even old ideas that work from somebody they trust. And, this is the really important part—People have their epiphanies when they have them, and you can't make people change their mindsets or behavior or have those epiphanies until they are ready.

On my call with our CEO, I suggested a simple solution. Let's send a short letter of invitation out to the senior executives in our target companies. All this letter was going to say was that The Gallup Organization had spent all these years collecting mountains of data and studying business problems of every stripe, and we had learned plenty that might be valuable to you, Mr. Executive. Let us share it with you. Yes, completely free of charge.

Our CEO couldn't believe it.

"What? No sales language in the letter?"

No.

"We're just going to invite people to join us and learn from us, and that's it?"

Yes.

He was incredulous. He then made a funny gesture that made us both laugh out loud. He suggested that we try this gambit only in Texas so if it didn't work we could say that we had only lost one state (albeit a really big one). And, he ended our short phone conversation by giving me this challenge, "If five people join this New Discoveries group, Dennis, it will be the best marketing idea we have ever had."

I started trembling a little and thinking about which five people I could get to join...my mom, my brother, my wife, etc.

But my fears turned out to be totally unfounded, because we sent out the letters one day to around 1,000 Texas senior executives, and in just a few days the New Discoveries emails started rolling in. One after another, executives and decision-makers joined our little troupe, and soon we had over 150 souls, all waiting on a note or white paper from us. After assembling this little "congregation," I started to work on what "sermons" to preach to each of them. I'd see in the business section of the daily paper that company A had a turnover problem, and I would send my contact at that company a white paper or sometimes I would have our engagement experts write a few paragraphs about how employee engagement correlates with turnover. Never did we ask for a meeting or offer to sell anything.

Never ever.

And, then one day, it would magically happen. An epiphany. After sometimes months of emails and white papers and articles, something would happen and the last bit of info we'd send over would just gently push them over the edge and they'd send a note back asking *me* for a meeting. "Could you send your guys out on Tuesday? You all obviously know more than we do about this stuff, so come help us out."

Now, *that* is the true definition of a warm client meeting. Those get-togethers were always cordial and kind and about as productive as it gets. Everybody was at church on time and glad to be there, metaphorically speaking.

And, there were some pleasant surprises. For almost 12 months, I sent emails and white papers and information and who knows what all to a company whose whole persona said "Go away!" But one day, the strangest thing happened. I got a call from a complete stranger, someone who was *not* on my New Discoveries roster, a senior executive who introduced himself and then proceeded to tell me how much he *loved* what I had been sending and how they did have the tiniest little turnover issue, and that he just *might* want to talk to one of our senior partners about how to fix it.

I couldn't help but ask, "Who are you and how did you know about us and how to contact me?"

His response floored me, "You didn't know? One of our lower level employees signed up for the New Discoveries and he has been forwarding them to *everyone in the company for the entire year!* Everyone from the CEO to the guy who sweeps the floors gets your emails and we've really all learned a lot from you guys."

What???? Can you say that in my good ear?

So, what's the lesson here? One lesson is that urgency happens when it happens, but you can help it along by figuring out what matters to your audience. The second lesson—If you can take the time to figure that out, you have a chance to get their attention, but it might not happen on the first or second try. It will happen when it happens. Be consistent. Be patient. Keep knocking on doors and caring. People will someday come to your "church." I can almost guarantee it.

> Urgency happens when it happens, but you can help it along by figuring out what matters to your audience. The second lesson—If you can take the time to figure that out, you have a chance to get their attention, but it might not happen on the first or second try. It will happen when it happens. Be consistent. Be patient. Keep knocking on doors and caring. People will someday come to your "church." I can almost guarantee it.

## John Maxwell

Toward the end of my glorious time at The Gallup Organization I had a chance to do some other things. It's one of the great things about being in a fast moving company…there's always lots to do and most likely not enough people to do it all. I became a senior staff writer for Gallup's flagship publication and spent some time interviewing our top clients and telling their stories in print. Loved it! My family and I also moved to Georgia and I went to work for the best boss I ever had—Ron Balmer—tremendous guy who really wanted to see his people grow.

One day, I got a call from our CEO, and he began the conversation by asking me if I was a "Jesus man."

I answered "yes, as a matter of fact I *am* a Jesus man."

"Well, good," he said. "Because we need one of those. We plan to take all this stuff we do for Best Buy, AT&T, and others and bring it to churches and denominations so they can be more effective. And, we want you to head up the marketing on that. You interested?"

It was a rhetorical question. Of course, I was interested.

Within a very few days of that decision, I got a call out of a clear blue sky from a young lady who worked with John Maxwell's organization. John is a superstar in the management consulting and speaking business, a never-ending idea generator and observer who has done *very well*. This young lady began by saying that she heard we had started this new part of The Gallup Organization and she wondered if we might like to rent a booth at one of John's events in Los Angeles. Oh, there were a few caveats and stipulations. We couldn't sell any books there, we could only give away a few books and business cards, and we could have conversations with people who attended.

I thought, what the heck? Why not try it? My wife went with me and we drove across town and finally got to this big mega-church where the event was being held. It was the night before the event and it took a while, but I finally found my little hovel, a small wooden desk in a corner, sort of out of the way. (It was kind of pathetic; something you might make in a high school woodshop class). I tacked up my little Gallup sign and laid out all 25 books I brought with me and my business cards, and that little table was totally filled to the edges. I looked across at John's table and it appeared to be 100-yards long with a library of books and video tapes, and even a John Maxwell Bible. Holy cow!

The next morning I showed up for the event and dutifully took my position behind my little desk, and then…oh my goodness, there were throngs of people who came out to sit at the feet of John Maxwell and hear his wisdom. There were at least 1,500 people there that day, and they all filed in and sat in rapt attention, as he spent the morning talking about how best to build a great team.

Soon, it was time for the lunch break, and I decided that I should walk down to the stage and meet John Maxwell. This was going to be my only chance, and Lord knows there wasn't enough activity at my little partial booth to worry about leaving it for a few minutes. I figured I would have at most 10 seconds to get his undivided attention. He was busy signing books for people and talking with them, and I dutifully stood in line pondering what to say.

When it came my turn, I shook his hand and said "Hi John. My name is Dennis Welch, and I'm with The Gallup Organization, and we're test driving one of these booths out there to see if we want to do any more of these events with you. I've been listening all morning to you talk about teamwork, and it makes me wonder if we at Gallup are not your competition."

He whirled around in his seat and faced me head on. I had his undivided attention, now.

"Are you?" he asked, in a very serious tone.

I said, "No, as a matter of fact, John, we're not. You've talked all morning about knowing your team, but how can that happen really? I've worked with people for years and not really known them. Thankfully, Gallup has developed a tool called the StrengthsFinder that can help you accurately measure each team member's strengths, so you won't have to guess about those things."

He got very quiet. I continued to the finish line: "And, we've written a book called Living Your Strengths that allows the reader to take the StrengthsFinder."

"Really?" he asked. "Well, by all means bring me two of those books to read, please. And, thank you."

What happened next is kind of crazy. After the lunch the audience reassembled. A young lady began doing an advertisement of sorts about John Maxwell's books and DVDs and so forth, and I stood in the back of the auditorium carefully watching the proceedings. Then I noticed that way in the back of the stage under a very dim light, John Maxwell was reading and flipping through the pages of a book he was obviously very taken with. When the young lady finished her commercial, I found out exactly what book had so captured his interest because he walked to the edge of the stage, and then he held up a copy of... *Living Your Strengths* and began:

"I didn't write this book, but I sure wish I had. During the lunch break today I spoke with Dennis Welch of the Gallup Organization, and he informed me that they have developed a tool called the StrengthsFinder, and that tool can help you accurately to know your team members. So, on the next break, I want everybody to go out into the lobby and find Dennis and buy a copy of this book from him."

Well, John certainly couldn't have known that I had only brought 25 books with me, and oh, by the way, I was told I couldn't sell *any*! But, he's The Master, and when he instructed 1,500 people to come see me on the next break, they literally *poured* out of the auditorium and, yes, they *did* find me. By the time the break was over my hovel and I were picked completely clean, no books, no cards, almost no clothes... crazy.

A couple of weeks later, I did another one of John's events, this time in Atlanta. Sometime during the day, his CEO came to my booth and asked me (incredulously), "Say, uh... did John Maxwell endorse your book in public at the L.A. event?"

"Yes. Yes he did."

"Well, I have to tell you, that has only happened this many times *ever*." (He was holding up just his index finger, the internationally known symbol for *once*.)

So, how did that happen? I had the privilege of listening to John all morning without speaking or interrupting him even once. I was a very interested spectator, sat and listened intently, and gleaned what was important to him from his talk. He really does care about organizations building great teams; it was obvious. Once I heard the morning half of his day-long talk, I knew beyond a shadow of a doubt what mattered to him. And then, I took all that info and condensed it into a 10-15 second opening line that started *the* conversation.

By the way, we wound up doing all of John Maxwell's events that year, and he wound up selling copies of our book on his book table (a first as far as I know), and when the hardback version of *Living Your Strengths* came out, John wrote a beautiful endorsement for the book. A home run for everybody concerned, and it all came from effective communication and listening carefully to hear what matters to your audience.

## Hola.

In the early 90's Hispanics were becoming the largest minority in the U.S., and every company wanted to know what they were thinking, what cars they might buy, who they might vote for, etc.

So, when Gallup's leadership found out that I spoke a little Spanish, they asked me to launch a Hispanic interviewing team.

We started very small, and soon, we were rolling down the tracks toward what turned out to be a critical part of Gallup's work. I was designated "Director of Hispanic Interviewing," and had a young man working for me that was destined to be the greatest recruiter of people I have personally ever known—Carlos Vazquez, a newlywed, University of Houston student, and a fiery Cuban who hated Castro and had escaped to America as a boy. Carlos was driven and smart and he had charisma in huge bushel baskets.

One day, after Carlos officially became our recruiter at the Houston office, he and I set out to do an event at The University of Houston. I got there before Carlos, and went about setting up our iron table with the white table cloth and the snazzy Gallup banner in the University Center that was abuzz with kids, all of them ignoring me, walking past as if I were invisible. I pushed the little Gallup pencils I had brought around on the little table and wondered where Carlos was and why in the heck we were doing such a lame deal in the first place.

Carlos showed up and then, suddenly, everything changed. He got up on a chair and started "preaching" about Gallup and how it was a fantastic place to work, and how you could set your own flexible hours and make really good money and still go to school. Before long, people started thronging us and the crowds pressed against the little table that only a few minutes before was as cold and quiet as an autopsy room. People *really, really, really* wanted to get an application and the number to call to apply —nobody ignored Carlos.

Before long, we had a full-house of Spanish interviewers who did remarkable work. In my last year in the role, we conducted 120,000 interviews in Spanish, half of those in Latin America. It was an unbridled success, and I would contend that the words Carlos used to attract people were perhaps the most important part of making it work.

Carlos could even do miracles. One of our sales guys was unaware that Brazil did *not* speak Spanish, so he sold a million dollar deal to do market research there, thinking my Hispanic interviewing team and I would have this covered. When he called me, he told me triumphantly how glad he was that I had started Spanish interviewing at Gallup so that he could sell this really big deal way down there in Brazil.

I remember how quiet it got when I informed him that people in Brazil speak Portuguese.

"Say…what?"

"Yep. Portuguese. Not Spanish."

"Then, you'd better figure out what we're gonna do. Get out there and hire a soccer team."

I relayed that conversation to Carlos and he wasn't rattled at all. In fact, we had a good laugh about it, right before he went out and hired an entire church filled with Brazilians, including the pastor. They were the greatest people you would ever want to work with and somehow Carlos was able to convince them to come to work with us to save this guy's bacon (and mine). They were stunningly good at this work, and the project went off without a hitch.

Words are magic. Don't forget that….

## *The Power of* WHO—**Bob Beaudine** **and** *The Today Show*

*Sports Illustrated* has called Bob Beaudine "the most influential man in sports you've never heard of." He is a recruiter. No, he is one of *the* recruiters of any kind, anywhere. But his specialty is sports. And, he's at the top of his game, so to speak. One of the best. If a professional or college coach or general manager, or a college athletic director gets fired or quits, the first call, many times is to Bob to start looking for their replacement. Bob is a multi-talented person, and he is one of the most energetic people I have ever known. He is also a stickler for detail which is just one reason he is terrific at his work.

The other reason is something he has written a bestselling book about. He calls it *The Power of* WHO. His thesis is that we all have a circle of true friends who love us and will do practically anything for us with no strings attached. But sadly, most of us have not "declared" our friendship to these people, and thus are not reaping the rich benefits of deep friendship.

Bob's book on the subject, *The Power of WHO—You Already Know Everyone You Need To Know*, came out right during the onset of the recession in 2009, and there were a lot of people out there who could really use a friend. Bob often quotes the statistic that 85 percent of all jobs come from just one phone call from a friend.

So, in Bob's mind, networking is, in his words, "crap." Useless. A waste of time and effort. His way—*The Power of Who* way—is more work. It requires us to declare our friendship, and it means that we have to take time to invest in the lives of our *who*.

When I first met Bob, I knew right away that we would be friends. We met at the offices of his agent, Jan Miller, and we all sat around a table and talked. Well, mostly Bob talked, and the more he talked the more fascinated I became with his *Power of WHO* idea. It was pure genius, and it could be really big and it could become a movement. I wanted to be a part of it.

At the time I was working with Barbara Cave Henricks at Cave Henricks Communications. We signed on to do the publicity on *The Power of WHO,* and right away the most amazing thing happened that proved that Bob was really on to something. Of course, Bob knew someone at NBC, and so did I. My contact was one of the senior producers there at *The Today Show,* and Bob knew a senior exec at the broadcasting company. Bob's friend wanted to get him on *The Today Show,* and so we triangulated our efforts. I went to my contact there and suggested that she meet with Bob the next time he was in New York City. I told her that if she spent 15 minutes with him, she would fall madly in love with his ideas, and would want to have him on the show. It also helped our argument that the unemployment numbers were horrendous and *The Power of WHO* had the possibility of remedying that for many.

Bob's message is a hopeful one, and at that time there was a huge shortage of hope on the job front. All of these ingredients went into the publicity stew, and Bob went off to New York to The Heisman presentation, and to meet with the producer at *The Today Show.* She was actually going to give Bob 15 minutes to explain the *Power of WHO* to her, and I was on pins and needles. He went in to her office at around 6 Eastern

Time, and I was on my way to a songwriter night here in Austin. When I got to the venue, I sat in my car waiting for Bob to call, thinking he'd be calling anytime. His 15 minutes were up a long time ago.

Eventually, I had to go in to the gig and get set up. Right before I went on stage, my phone rang, and it was Bob. It had been an hour and half!

"What in the world happened in there, Bob?"

"Well," he began, "I think it went well."

"Go on. Please."

"She cried. And, she hugged me as I left. That's probably a good sign, right?" he asked with a little understatement.

Yes, it was a good sign, as it turned out. They booked Bob for January 15, and we all flew to New York for the show—he and I and his sweet wife and two of his beautiful daughters. We had dinner the night before, Bob smoked a cigar, and we had an amazing evening. Ann Curry would be interviewing him the next morning.

Kind of unbelievable, really. But miracles do happen, and we were about to see another one.

Toward the end of that evening, Bob made an interesting comment that turned out to be prophetic. "Wouldn't it be great if we could get three minutes with Ann Curry before the interview?"

"Yes, Bob, it would," I said. "But I'm not too sure about how to do that."

We all turned in early since the morning and *The Today Show* interview would come upon us very soon. I went back to my room and fell asleep and slept about 10 minutes and woke up with an idea—what if we arrived at the NBC Studios 30 minutes earlier than scheduled and just took our chances? I called Bob in his hotel room and suggested that, and he agreed that it was a good idea and probably our only chance to get three minutes with Ann.

We had our car pick us up the next morning 30 minutes early, and off we went, not knowing really what to expect. We had no sooner gotten into the green room there, when the young segment producer walked in, greeted us, and asked, "Would you all like to be on the set when Mr. Beaudine does his interview?"

Another rhetorical question.

We all walked out into the hallway and Bob grabbed me by the sleeve and said "This is going to happen isn't it?"

What happened next can only be chalked up to a God who loves us and really does care about the details of our lives here on earth. Ann Curry finished the interview she was doing when we walked on to the set; then she walked straight over, greeted all of us, and said, "Bob, it sure would be great if we had a few minutes to chat before our interview."

> The lesson here? Yes, we live in a world of email and texts. But, sometimes you have to ride in and tell your story. And, you have to tell it so that people will be drawn into it. You may only have 15 minutes (if you're lucky), and there better not be a wasted word.

Well, after we picked our jaws up off the floor, Bob walked over and sat down with her and they started talking. Right before Ann interviewed Bob on national TV, she told him that they would have to stop talking because he was going to make her cry. She already loved Bob and his book.

Then, the lights and cameras came up, and they together conducted an interview that was about as good as it gets. The book rocketed up Amazon's sales chart, and more importantly, a whole throng of new "parishioners" joined *The Power of WHO* "church."

Afterward, Ann asked us to stick around and sit on *The Today Show* couch and visit for a while. She was gracious and kind, and it was truly unforgettable.

The lesson here? Yes, we live in a world of email and texts. But, sometimes you have to ride in and tell your story. And, you have to tell it so that people will be drawn into it. You may only have 15 minutes (if you're lucky), and there better not be a wasted word.

Nobody does it better than Bob Beaudine. And, because of that, the *Power of WHO* movement continues today, as strong as ever.

## *You. According to Them*—Sara Canaday

Let me begin by saying that I *love* this book, and Sara Canaday, the author, is one of the brightest people that I know. I was also immediately drawn to the title: *You—According to Them*. How could you not love that?

The book is about the blind spots we all have. For example, we think we're driven and decisive, and others we work with just think we're jerks. You know what I mean? Ever work with somebody, or *for* somebody who has no idea that they are running everybody off, and they justify their behavior by basically not seeing how awful it is and what they are inflicting on the people around them. They get decent results in spite of their behavior, and somehow that justifies it all in their minds.

The notion that we all have blind spots is a great one, and Sara totally nailed it in this book. In my opinion, every manager and leader in America should read *You—According to Them* and then they should buy a copy for everybody that reports to them. This is a real problem in workplaces everywhere; Sara lays out the issues in detail and then prescribes the fixes for each blind spot that she has identified.

The big question facing us when we began the publicity campaign was how do we make the media care about this problem today? The country was mired in a deep recession when the book came out, and it was hard to be heard over all the noise of the troubles we faced as a country. So, we had to figure out how to make it relevant. Remember the vitally important question: Why should I care about it *today*?

43

I decided that the Recession was going to be our friend, in a way. What self-respecting manager or leader would want to have his team functioning at less than 110 percent in this lousy economic environment? In most industries there were many layoffs, and skeleton crews left doing the lion's share of the work needed to be hitting on all cylinders. This was true in the media as well, by the way. Most daily papers were down to the smallest crew possible to get the work done and the paper published every day. Print media of all kinds were under siege. So, they would understand the problem better than anyone.

And that was my pitch.

When Sara and I started working together, I asked her (as I often do) what her dream outcome would be for our efforts. She created a media list that included *Forbes*, CNBC, *Success Magazine,* and The American Marketing Association. But, when she said that she wanted to be a regular contributor to *Psychology Today,* my heart sunk just a little. I didn't know anybody there, but I was certainly willing to try.

Try we did. Our four-month campaign went all the way down to the last two weeks before, completely out of nowhere, the editor of *PsychologyToday.com* emailed me with all the warmth she could muster. We had reached out to her and her associate for the entire campaign and yet it took almost the entire campaign and mounting evidence that others were interested in Sara's message before she decided to let her be a regular contributor. By the time she acquiesced, Sara was already a regular contributor to the *Huffington Post,* had written a piece for CNBC.com. and had other high profile successes.

Never give up, because you just don't know what great thing is right around the corner.

Stories like this are one of the reasons I love my job. I'm okay with silence and I never give up. In fact, I do a weekly activity report for my clients and the activity used to be divided between *Confirmed Interest, Pending Interest,* and *Declined.* But these days, my report only has *Confirmed* and *Pending,* and I have removed the *Declined* section altogether, and here's why. I assume that even if media contacts are ignoring my pitches currently, that eventually they will come around and see how important this is. And, even if they blatantly turn me down at the beginning of the campaign, I will continue to circle back to them throughout the remainder of our work and remind them that others are covering it. Time and again, I have seen campaigns start slow and build to a crescendo, and no two campaigns are alike.

Our campaign for *You—According to Them* set the bar pretty high and for the most part, by the time we had finished the campaign, we had met or exceeded our expectations, even after being rebuffed or ignored.

The lesson here? Never give up, because you just don't know what great thing is right around the corner.

## *Startup*—**Kevin Ready**

When I first started *Articulate*, I got a call from an author named Kevin Ready. Kevin had recently penned a book about starting a company, and it was all set to publish soon by a small New York publisher that was starting a business book division. He had heard from a mutual business acquaintance that I did book publicity, and he asked if I would meet him in South Austin at a Starbucks to discuss maybe working together on his new book. I remember thinking, when he described the book and  its subject to me over the phone, that this was going to be difficult because there are a lot of books already out there and soon to be out there about how to start companies. But, I agreed to meet with Kevin because I liked him immediately, and he sounded very credible and smart even in our brief phone exchange.

If I live to be a hundred, I'll never forget my meeting that afternoon with Kevin. We sat down at one of the outside tables and he started talking and describing some of the work he was doing and his ideas. It was like having a conversation with Michael Keaton's character in *Night Shift*. He needed a foil helmet to keep all of the ideas out! He was a literal font of creativity, obviously very smart, and he hadn't shaved in a couple of days and looked sort of disheveled at first glance. But while he was talking about all of this fascinating stuff that he dreamed of doing and that he was currently involved with…it hit me. This campaign was not going to be primarily about the book. It was going to be about *him!* We were going to answer the "Who's the messenger?" question in a way that would intrigue media contacts to want to know more about Kevin. That was the plan anyway.

I did my due diligence and set the publicity bar kind of low. I said, "Kevin, you're a first time author, and your publisher is a very small publisher, who up to now has put out books about things like your pulmonary system; so this is going to be hard. But I promise, I'll do the best I can."

I decided that I would start out by figuring out a nickname for him and I quickly settled on the "Mad Scientist of Entrepreneurs."

Kevin Ready is the "Mad Scientist of Entrepreneurs."

Crazy, eh?

Yes, kind of crazy, but it had a nice ring to it.

I wrote a press kit and pulled a media list and went to work. I went out with my pitches every week and told my media contacts that I had discovered the Mad Scientist of Entrepreneurs right here in Austin, Texas. For a while, we heard a lot of silence, and that was okay. That happens a lot in my business and it just means that you have to try again and again until you hear something. Again, you never give up, because in your heart you know that this guy has something to say, and he has as much right to say it as anybody else.

One night, out of the blue, I got an email from an editor at the *Wall Street Journal*, asking me if Kevin would be willing to be interviewed for a story that she was writing about starting a business, and wondered if the Mad Scientist of Entrepreneurs might be interested in being interviewed for it.

Are you kidding me? He'd be delighted. I knew that without even asking him. I set up the interview, and Kevin was spectacular, so much so that he was cited as an expert in the article. How crazy is that? Only a few weeks

> Soon, I got a call asking if Kevin would like to write his own article for *The Wall Street Journal,* giving his thoughts on starting a company from his own unique perspective.

before, he was a first time author putting out a little book about starting a company, and now he's an *expert?*

Incredible. But we weren't done yet. Soon, I got a call asking if Kevin would like to write his own article for *The Wall Street Journal,* giving his thoughts on starting a company from his own unique perspective.

*Really?*

Though that was all very cool, we weren't done yet. One day, I got an email asking if Kevin would like to be a regular contributor to *Forbes.com,* and their small business channel on their highly trafficked site.

Yes. Yes, he would.

So, Kevin became a regular contributor to *Forbes* and you can find his *Ready For Business* blog there at: http://www.forbes.com/sites/kevinready/

I *loved* this campaign—it proved once and for all that if you describe the messenger in the right terms, and you tell the truth about them in a way that intrigues people who have probably heard it all before, you can make things happen that should *not* be happening.

The only thing I wish I had done that I didn't was to get a picture of Kevin in front of the whiteboard he keeps in his office. This board stretches clear across the room and has square roots, formulae, and who knows what all on it, as if the guy is going to the moon. If a picture is really worth a thousand words, then, if we had posed him in front of that thing with a couple of days of whiskers and unkempt hair, I wouldn't have needed to say a single word, because everyone who saw it would say—"yep, that must be that Mad Scientist of Entrepreneurs I keep hearing about."

## *Finding Work*

I'm an optimist, but even this one took me by surprise. When I worked at The Gallup Organization, we had an amazing writer and researcher named Roger Wright, who I became good friends with. He actually co-wrote a manuscript with best-selling author Curt Coffman about customer service, and I thought it was the best written book we had ever written at Gallup. Unfortunately, the book was written but never actually published.

One day, Roger called me and said that he was working on a manuscript for a book about jobs. I was immediately thinking "oh, no, not another 1-2-3, pull these levers and get a job book. That's another subject that has been beat to death in the book business." But, because Roger is such a wonderful writer, I was curious to read it. I actually was already pretty sure that I would not take the book.

Then the manuscript landed in my mailbox, and I started reading it and… I couldn't put it down. It was as far from a 1-2-3-get-a-job book as it could be. It was filled with stories and powerful anecdotes that made the reader think about their talents and gifts, what their communities needed, and how they could use those talents and gifts to fill those needs.

After reading the book, I agreed to take it, mainly because it fits into my philosophy for what we do as a company. If it doesn't change the world for the better, at least a little, I'm not interested. I don't want to take projects because we need the business or to keep the lights on. This work is difficult enough when you are fully vested in a book or idea. It's darn near impossible when you are just going through the motions. Why? Because your targets can sense that you are not excited about it, just as they can sense when you are very enthusiastic about an idea or an author.

## A Word about Hurdles

I've decided that all great endeavors that change the world start out with one thing in common—seemingly insurmountable hurdles. This campaign was no exception. Right at the onset, I got an email from a syndicated jobs columnist who asked if I had any jobs experts on my client list who would be willing to write a couple of paragraphs about finding work. She suggested that maybe it should be something not typical, and new fresh ideas that were out of the box. Well, Roger Wright has never been in the box, ever. I thought this might be an opportunity to jump-start the campaign at the outset, so I asked him to write a few paragraphs for this person.

Let's just say that the response was tepid at best and outright negative, if we want to honestly appraise it. Basically this syndicated columnists said that Roger was a nut, a "wack-job" who didn't really understand the job-hunting process at all and was even a bit out of touch with reality. What does he mean that the job-hunting process was not linear? What does that even mean?

So, our campaign began with one of the top jobs experts in the media saying Roger didn't know what he was talking about. In a way, I should have expected it. But, it blindsided me, and I was very discouraged by her response.

We pressed on with our publicity campaign as if nothing like that had ever happened. I started reaching out to the smaller targets to see if we could generate any interest at all. We needed a little toehold if we were planning to climb the mountain.

One day, after a prolonged period of silence in the campaign, a free-lancer, Dawn Klingensmith, emailed me and said she'd like to talk with Roger about *The Five*—his five organizing principles around finding work. I set up the interview and Dawn called Roger. Sure enough, she got what he was talking about in a way that no one in the media had up to that time. She wrote a terrific piece that wound up being syndicated, and soon it appeared in the *Philadelphia Inquirer,* among other dailies around the country.

But, Dawn wasn't done yet. She called Roger again and talked about another one of *The Five,* and sure enough it, too, appeared in dailies around the country.

I could feel the wheels of the campaign beginning to lift off the runway. These moments are my favorite moments in my work. After all the pitching and work and messaging, somebody or several somebodies start writing about the book and the author. It's pure elation, quite honestly. I feel like I've won the lottery.

After Dawn's articles ran, a nationally syndicated radio show decided that they would let Roger be interviewed and that interview ran on 150 stations around the country.

All of this activity confirmed what I already knew: Roger apparently wasn't crazy after all, and his unique and completely original ideas were gaining traction.

And, it kept getting better. Next, CNBC.com ran a guest column that Roger penned, and that was picked up by Yahoo Finance before that day was over.

Then, I pitched Roger and the book to *Forbes,* and it started to get really interesting. My contact there read the press kit and apparently looked at Roger's other national articles and exposure and said that they were "intrigued." Within an hour, one of *Forbes'* top writers called me and asked if she could speak to Roger directly.

By the way, for the uninitiated, the answer to that question is always an enthusiastic YES!

I connected her with Roger at home and she interviewed him for an hour or so. Then, all day long she kept circling back to him on email and asking follow-up questions.

Along about five o'clock that afternoon I got a call from Roger that I'll never forget. He said "You know, Dennis, either I'm a genius or I'm the biggest and most self-delusional charlatan in the universe, based on her questions. She says the story will run tomorrow, and I guess we'll all find out together what she thinks about me and my independently published book."

If you get a chance, go to Forbes.com and read the story: http://www.forbes.com/sites/susanadams/2013/04/03/5-ways-to-find-work-when-there-are-no-jobs/#

Honestly, we could have written it ourselves and it would not have been more positive. She totally got it. The hurdle we ran into at the beginning of the campaign was now so far back in our rearview mirror that it was hardly visible at all.

We finished Roger's campaign with a flurry. He is a prolific writer and blogger and one of his dreams was to be a regular contributor to *The Huffington Post*. He also wanted to do a book signing in his hometown of Chicago, and be on WGN-TV.

Every single one of those things happened for him, and I couldn't be happier. He's a good friend, and I understand his mission and the potential it has to change lives and offer hope to people around the country.

I loved being a part of it for a while.

> Don't let the critics take you down. Never settle, never try to fit your ideas into somebody else's narrow view of what they should be. You can't win like that. Be yourself. Be original. Be proud of being your own person and creating something that adds to the conversation, whatever that conversation may be.

Here's an important takeaway from this experience for all of us: Don't let the critics take you down. Never settle, never try to fit your ideas into somebody else's narrow view of what they should be. You can't win like that. Be yourself. Be original. Be proud of being your own person and creating something that adds to the conversation, whatever that conversation may be.

# The Magic
# of Choosing
# the Right Words

Sometimes, writers just get it right. And, not only do they get it right, they make it look easy. Great writers of all kinds do that.

I think it's good to see other communicators hit it out of the park, because it reminds us of what's possible every time we set out to start important conversations. I think we've established that literally, anything is possible if we get it right—yes?

I think every writer at one time or another has moments of panic when they look at the blank page and think about what they want to say to start this mysterious and profound process. Sometimes, they even have a more severe version of that panic, called writer's block. But, the great ones press on, working through the valleys and eventually they end up on the mountaintop. And, when they do, they touch us in a way that we cannot really get over. The great writers end up parsing every word and every phrase, and they leave no stone unturned in an effort to get it as close to perfect as they can. They write things and walk away for a while to let what they have written simmer and stew.

> I think it's good to see other communicators hit it out of the park, because it reminds us of what's possible every time we set out to start important conversations. I think we've established that literally, anything is possible if we get it right—yes?

It's interesting, that most everyone can physically write, but there are only a precious few who pen the words that become etched forever into the public psyche, part of our culture, and history. Abraham Lincoln wrote the *Gettysburg Address* thinking that no one would really remember it down the road. And, yet, we know now that it is one of the great speeches of all time. And, it's not very long. He used an economy of words, like great writers do. None wasted.

That should be our benchmark, the bar we shoot for. Most of us will surely *not* write the *Gettysburg Address*, but we can do our best work that we are capable of given our talents and skills. We should strive to write our *Gettysburg Address*, whatever that may be.

Greatness is possible, and you never know when it's going to happen. Be patient. Parse every word. Re-think and edit. If you do, something amazing can happen.

Let's talk a little more about what greatness looks like. I'm using a couple of my favorite examples of word magic. You probably have different ones that you think of when you are setting the bar for verbal and written excellence.

## Over the Rainbow

My grandkids love *The Wizard of Oz*. Every time they stay at our house we wind up watching it again as if we had never seen it before. It is so well done that I always glean something new from it when I see it again. Sitting in my living room with my grandkids and a bowl of popcorn doesn't hurt either.

For almost 80 years now, Dorothy has walked out to the hay bale on her Kansas farm and sung the famous and well-chosen words to *Over the Rainbow*. We all relate somehow to them, don't we? But just think about those weary souls who first heard them. It was 1939, and throngs gathered together in theaters around the world to get away from the struggles of the day. The Depression had sapped the life out of people far and wide, and there were wars and rumors of wars, and dictators, and an uncertain future for everyone. Yet there, on the silver screen, one of the world's biggest film stars sang longingly about a place where "troubles melt like lemon drops," and "happy little bluebirds fly." It ends with the question everyone in the audience was assuredly asking themselves in unison even before they ever bought a ticket and sat down in the padded seats that night: "Why, oh why can't I?"

It wasn't just the music that drew us into the story. Every word of the script was carefully crafted to elicit a particular response—love, anger, sadness. When Dorothy meets the wizard at the beginning of the film in his wagon, he plants the foundation for the story in her heart that the rest of the film rests upon. He tells her that Aunt Em "looks careworn" and is "holding her hand over her heart." We immediately understand those signals. Her beloved Aunt Em's in trouble.

Dorothy immediately decides to go home to check on her, but never really makes it there until the end of the film. The ranch hands go with her to Oz, and she even mentions (once she gets there and meets her traveling companions) that they look familiar, but then quickly dismisses it.

It's beautiful how it all unfolds with all the layers and layers of the story, each complicated and related thread woven into another, and all made to look so seamless. It feels like it was easy to write this film because it works so effortlessly, but this kind of writing and re-writing and laying out of the characters and their nuances is tedious and extremely difficult. So difficult, in fact, that very few people, relatively speaking, can make a living writing scripts. Like writing books and music, everyone thinks they could probably do it at a high level if called upon, but, not surprisingly, only a tiny shard of the population have the talent to do it in the first place, and an even tinier fraction of those people have honed their gift to such a fine edge that they can consistently produce scripts, songs, and books that live on in our hearts long after they are gone.

> Great writers know exactly what they are tasked with. They are assigned the sometimes unenviable and always complicated role of saying for us what we cannot say for ourselves. It's arduous and weighty work.

Great writers know exactly what they are tasked with. They are assigned the sometimes unenviable and always complicated role of saying for us what we cannot say for ourselves. It's arduous and weighty work, and sometimes all the effort pays off and sometimes it doesn't. Great songwriters that I know say they write 100 songs or more for every one that gets recorded. That means that 99 percent of their work winds up on the cutting room floor. It means every single word and phrase has to be parsed, cut, edited, and rewritten. They have to understand their audience completely and they have to think of them every second throughout the writing process.

But… when they get it right, we never get over it. Decades later, we hear a song that speaks to our broken hearts, our rebellion, or our joy, and it transports us back to the moment we first heard it and how it seared its way into our hearts.

## *Starry Starry Night:* **My Love Affair with Words and the Pictures They Can Create**

When I was 14, I heard Don McLean sing *Starry, Starry Night,* his brilliant ode to the troubled artist Vincent Van Gogh. I remember exactly where I was the day I heard it first. I was in my friend Jack Ellis' car and we were on our way to a church youth meeting in north Houston… I heard those opening lines and I was captured.

I remain so until this very day—

*Starry, Starry Night.*

*Paint your pallid blue and gray*

*Look out on a summer's day with eyes that know the darkness in my soul.*

The words burned into my brain and every single thing about them spoke to me. They were relentless, and each line that followed was like a tsunami of emotion. I found it hard to believe at the time that anyone could conjure up such beauty and create this kind of poetry, and I secretly longed to try that for myself.

Over the 40-plus years since, I have learned a little about what it takes to create that kind of beauty with just the right pictures painted with just the proper phrases and sentences. I know the hours it takes to hone a fine edge on a message—to build an emotional case that speaks to the listener or the reader and moves them.

It should be our constant quest to get it right. Why? Because every message and every listener is different and unique, and finding the key to their hearts and minds is a never-ending quest. These days, I do publicity for books and ideas that I care about deeply, and each book or idea is armed with only a very few unique hooks that will matter to the media person on the other end of the email trail. If I get it right, I get to bring something that changes the world a little bit to public attention so that it can run its course and start the conversations it was meant to start.

> Every message and every listener is different and unique, and finding the key to their hearts and minds is a never-ending quest.

You can do this, too, with your ideas and messages. In the next section, we'll start talking about how.

# Magic Ingredients

How do we get the message that matters—our message—through to the people we are trying to reach? My mentor in the book PR business, Barbara Henricks, says that there are really only three questions that our media target is asking when they get an email or a letter or call from us:

- What's the message?
- Who's the messenger?
- Why do I care about it today?

I would contend that those questions are in the minds of not just media targets, but every important target in every situation, and we must understand that our mission as "message senders" is really a simple one: answer these three vitally important questions. Period. Do so and you begin to change things; conversations start, the sales cycle can begin, people with good books, ideas, and products of all kinds can start sharing them with a wider audience.

Interestingly, the weight of these three questions is not always equally important. Sometimes who the messenger is turns out to be a lot more important than what the message is; sometimes who the messenger is also answers the "why should I care about it today?" question.

For example, when I worked with Doug Conant, former CEO of Campbell's Soup, it was the first time in all of my years of work trying to bring books to public attention that I actually had media people contacting me. People in the media found out that we were representing him and he was so highly thought of they expressed an immediate interest in having him on their shows, and interviewing him for their publications. Doug's book, *Touchpoints*, is a terrific book co-authored with Mette Norgaard, a brilliant consultant and Doug's good friend. It hit the *New York Times* bestseller list, and we went to New York for Doug and Mette to do numerous TV shows and print interviews. The messenger was almost so important here that the other two questions became irrelevant; at least as it impacted whether or not they would be having them on their shows and bringing attention to the book. Doug in particular is so revered and so highly thought of that the media, in essence, trusted him to answer the other two questions. It was a very successful campaign, and I felt like I made a couple of good friends in the process.

But, let's take a look at each individual question and discuss each one for a minute or two.

## What's the Message?

It is difficult to take really complex ideas that are numerous and profound enough to fill a book, and boil them down to an elevator speech or an executive summary. But this is important to know: *Every* message, no matter how complicated or arcane, has a few "hooks" hidden somewhere inside, and those "hooks" are the most important part of getting attention from people who have too many suitors, too many messengers at the door, each thinking their message and messenger is *most* important.

To begin with, it's a gift of sorts to be able to read an entire book, peruse a mountain of research, or explain a suite of products for sale, and then find the nuggets that you *know* will matter to your audience. Finding a concise and yet still effective way of describing and delivering those nuggets is critical to getting the attention and response you seek.

> *Every* message, no matter how complicated or arcane, has a few "hooks" hidden somewhere inside, and those "hooks" are the most important part of getting attention from people who have too many suitors, too many messengers at the door, each thinking their message and messenger is *most* important.

If you can't keep it relatively concise you're probably dead in the water and going nowhere. Have you ever gotten emails from people who have no filter and no idea what's important so they just send everything? The lights dim when the email comes over and you sigh because you know that every thought that entered the sender's head during the wiring of this massive and unfocused epic will be in that note somewhere; you also know that you just might as well sit down and kick your shoes off because this is going to take a while. The bad news? At the end of all this gibberish you may still not know why they sent it or why you should care. Just think if you worked for CNBC or the *New York Times*. No wonder they are such a tough audience, and getting their attention is so complicated and seemingly impossible sometimes.

You don't have to be a book publicist or even in the PR business to deal with these problems. You have customers, right? You have business associates, yes? You communicate with them (or try) every day; maybe several times a day. Guess what? Those people are mentally scrolling through those three questions with every email or phone call they receive from you.

Notice that the question is *not* What's *a* message. Rather, it's What's *the* message. Get this part wrong and there'll be no conversation starting around your great idea or product. You'll be nuked with the spam and left in the dead-letter box along with all the people who think that if they just include everything, they are bound to have something that matters to you in there somewhere.

Big mistake. And getting bigger, because people are getting busier and there are more ways to be distracted and communicated with than ever. There's too much noise, so concisely telling me what the message is and keeping in mind what part of it I will care most about most is critical.

## Who's the Messenger?

Well, it sure helps when you're working with Doug Conant, Bill Clinton, or Jack Welch. The 'Who's the messenger?' question overrides everything and people are clamoring to hear what these people have to say.

But what if you are a first time author, nobody famous, but you have a great idea and you really deserve a wider audience? Somehow, I have to make hard-bitten news people and editors believe that is true about you, and I have to tell you that it is by far the hardest thing I do. But, I totally *love* doing it! I get a kick out of finding those who are for now unknown and helping them find their audience. In some ways, it is what I feel called to do—what I was put on this earth for.

I begin that quest to figure out the pitch, the message I will be sending out to the media, by doing something that sounds counterintuitive at first glance: we re-write the author's bio. And, I have my own way of doing that. I call you up and ask you ten to twelve open-ended questions and I record your answers. Then, I sit down and transcribe every word by hand, the old-fashioned way, with an ink pen and a legal pad. My sons were appalled when they first heard this travesty, that I was actually transcribing recorded interviews *by hand*! "Dad," they said (practically screaming), "what's with you? Did you know that there are programs that will transcribe it all for you?"

Well, yes I do know, but quite honestly it wouldn't matter. Because I am fishing for the hooks in your personal story, and amazingly I always find them.

Always.

Always.

I've had people push back and say "My life's not interesting…"

But they were wrong. All of us have interesting lives, though the details may not be interesting to us.

I would contend that this can happen for literally anyone, anywhere, anytime. Later on in this little book, I'll tell some real-life stories of first-time authors who found themselves in the national spotlight simply because we successfully answered the "Who's the messenger" question to the satisfaction of those who could swing open the curtains and bring these deserving people and their books and ideas out onto The Big Stage. That makes my day and it never gets old. I don't need

> All of us have interesting lives, though the details may not be interesting to us.

the spotlight, but I love it when it happens for you. Step one is to figure out what it is about you that will intrigue people enough to check you out.

## Why Should I Care about It Today?

This question is really about just one thing—urgency. I think we've established that people are busy, have a lot of noise, and lots of choices to take their attention away from you and your message. They may love the messenger, and they may even be drawn to the message, but if you can't tell them in no uncertain terms why they should care about it *today*, then, they are done here and they are on to the next thing.

Creating urgency can come in a lot of forms, but let's talk about just two of them. One is connecting your message and messenger to a current event or problem to be solved. You, your client, or your company have the answer, and we needed answers yesterday, so I'm interested. I have a problem that I can't solve and you can help me solve it. I'm all ears.

> You can't fall back on your tried-and-true taxonomy. You have to take the time to find a verbal bridge that allows your audience to get on board with you.

I think the most common enemy of answering this question successfully is being insular and using taxonomy that we understand but that is completely foreign to our listeners. Remember, we live what we do every day and it becomes commonplace; thus our conversations with each other about what we do takes on a language all its own. In fact, just recently I was on a call with a new client who used acronyms and abbreviations and terms that totally stopped the conversation for me. Remember, you have to think about your audience, many (or perhaps most) of whom are not among the initiated regarding your product, idea, or service. You can't fall back on your tried-and-true taxonomy. You have to take the time to find a verbal bridge that allows your audience to get on board with you.

That's very hard to do. I grew up in the church, a shining example of insular thinking. Back then, we used terms about Christianity that only we understood. And, then we wondered why people didn't want to become Christians. When I started writing songs, I tried very hard to paint verbal pictures about real issues that my listener could understand and relate to. It was a hundred times harder to do that than to fall back on the familiar.

But, let me assure you, you can get some amazing conversations started about your "church" if you figure out how to make what you do relatable and understandable.

## Telling Your "Who's the Messenger" Story—A Word about Bios and Why They Matter

We live in a two-dimensional world much of the time. Websites are in many cases replacing brick-and-mortar stores, and texting has replaced real conversation and interchange. But here's what I believe: we have *not* changed as people. We still love a great story, we like doing business with people that we at least think we know, and somehow we have to achieve that in an ever-changing world.

Let me give you an example. One time, right after I left The Gallup Organization and started my own company, I interviewed a young lady to write her bio. She had worked with me at Gallup and had gone out on her own to start a very successful real estate company in Houston. She liked the result of that exercise so much that she asked me to write one for her mother, who also worked with her at the real estate company. Instead of doing the interview by phone, I drove out their offices and sat down in a conference room with her and took out my recorder to start the interview; sure enough she put up her hand and asked me to stop before we ever got started, really.

"Listen," she said, "my life is not very interesting, and I hate to waste your time."

I said, "Would you please let me be the judge of that?"

She agreed, and we began the interview; I have to tell you it was one of the most interesting interviews I have ever done. It turns out that this lady and her daughter escaped from Cuba during the Mariel boatlift, and they were incarcerated for months in Arkansas when they first arrived in America. The camp in which they were locked up was filled with crazy people and criminals. She had to leave relatives behind in Cuba in order to give her daughter a chance at a better life.

Somewhere in her story, she offered the *hook:* " I love selling houses she said... not for the money, but because I feel somehow that every time I sell a house to people who can afford houses, I am somehow making up for the people in Cuba who cannot."

*Boom!* You hear that sound? That's the sound of the phone ringing and people knocking down this lady's door when they read that she doesn't sell houses because she's trying to get rich. Her mission for why she sells houses is relatable and attractive. We put her bio on the site and immediately her business exploded. The "Who's the messenger" question was answered with a resounding response that set her apart from all other realtors that people could have chosen.

It's funny, almost everyone that I do these bio interviews with starts out by telling me that this probably won't be terribly interesting. But here's the truth. Though our lives may not be very interesting to us, they just might be fascinating to others. That is one really good reason, by the way, that, as a rule, we shouldn't write our own bios.

How do I do it? As I said, I start with those ten to twelve open-ended questions that I ask in a phone interview. I encourage the subject to talk a lot about each one of the questions, and suggest that more is so much better than less when doing these things. I record the interview, and then I go back and transcribe it by hand.

Yes, with a pen and a piece of paper. The old-fashioned way.

Here's what happens when you do that. You get to hear what people really care about. If you listen carefully, you'll hear the timbre of their voices change at the appropriate time. You get to hear the *why*. You have a chance to figure out how they got here to this role, why they stay here, and why they love it so.

That's attractive stuff, and it's a piece that's sorely missing in our two-dimensional world. People discount their own stories and it's sometimes painfully obvious. I picked up a real estate magazine in a local grocery store recently and every page was the same: a picture of a person, pictures of houses, a red background, a white frame around the house pictures. Nothing differentiated one seller from the next. I could only tell that they had a head, they had a phone, and they had houses for sale. I wasn't drawn to them.

People like doing business with people that they think they know. That has always been so, and it is not likely to change. Our stories about ourselves and our work have to do the work that used to happen in person when people walked into our stores or offices. We have to make them care about us, trust us, and even like us.

See below, a few of my favorite bios with a little back story of each.

## Greg Cootsona

Greg Cootsona is a remarkable guy with many talents and gifts. I worked on his first book, *Say Yes to NO,* published by Doubleday. He is a pastor, gifted writer and speaker, and a C.S. Lewis-kind of Christian thinker. He's also a drummer and a musician. I tried to convey all of that in this one-page story.

# About Greg Cootsona

Greg Cootsona has always been intrigued by the rhythms of life. From his earliest days growing up in Menlo Park, California, to his sojourn as a pastor in New York City, he has always striven to better understand how life is to be lived and how we can be at our best for the work we are called to do and for those we love.

In his youth, Greg loved the rhythm of tennis and was one of the top players in his state. His family was very supportive and would even take days off from their jobs to get him to and from important tournaments. "My mother was my first PR agent," he says. "She was always happy to talk about me to others." But by the time he was twelve, he had lost interest in tennis, feeling the work involved wasn't worth the outcome.

Then, Greg began to play drums and discovered the joy of music. Throughout his teen years he played in one of the best-known high school jazz and big band outfits in the country and even played the main stage at Monteux, all before turning eighteen. He had always liked school, but he really fell in love with learning in his junior and senior years, before entering UC Berkeley and finding that "there was this terrific interplay of ideas, and I wasn't really sure what *my idea* was. I was really interested in the big questions that had confounded humanity down through the years— Philosophy, Sociology, Literature, etc. So I chose Literature."

But somewhere in his quest to answer the big questions, he was blinded by a light so profound and so bright that it could not be ignored, and that experience changed his life forever. He was exposed to Christianity in a way that he had never before experienced and, as he had done with tennis and music, he did his due diligence. He began to investigate as fully as he knew how this life that so many intellectuals down through the ages had chosen. "I started reading *Mere Christianity* by C.S. Lewis, and it really got under my skin," he admits. "What drew me was the person of Christ, but I also found it to be the most compelling lifestyle. It brought coherence and meaning to my life in a way that nothing else did."

After receiving his doctorate in 1996, Greg took a full-time position at the prestigious Fifth Avenue Presbyterian Church in New York City. It was there that the rhythms of life became a bit too intense, and a brush with heart trouble and high blood pressure led him to examine his (and as it turns out, *our*) priorities. The result of that examination was his book, *Say Yes To NO*, published by Random House in March '09.

His mission is really a simple one and he pursues that mission with great vigor and joy whether he is teaching a class, playing the drums, or writing a book: "to enjoy the love of God and to glorify Him with the use of my time, my creative passion and gifts for the good of those around me, and ultimately for the good of all humankind."

Greg currently lives in Chico, California and is the Associate Pastor of Adult Discipleship and College Ministries at Bidwell Presbyterian Church. He is married to Laura, and they have two daughters Melanie and Elizabeth.

## Babette Hughes

Babette Hughes is a remarkable person on many levels. She is 90 years old as of this writing, and she has just finished writing her second novel, and is well on her way to writing her third. She has also written a memoir about her fascinating life. She has loads of credibility, and she is a truly great writer, in my opinion. She should be an encouragement to many who feel that they are too old and have been put out to pasture to languish and be unproductive for the rest of their lives.

I am doing the publicity on her novel. *The Red Scarf*, the follow-up to *The Hat*. Both are riveting stories of gangsters and guns and the people involved. Babette makes her women strong in her stories, as it should be. They are survivors, and they are unforgettable characters.

Her first nationally published piece was for *The Saturday Review* way back in 1963.

I wanted my media contacts who might write about her or the book to know all of this quickly. I wanted to be sure that all of this really cool stuff about her did not get lost in the shuffle of details that you often find in press kits.

I open the press kit with: *Nonagenarian novelist Babette Hughes has done it again. She has penned a powerful follow-up to The Hat, award-winning acclaimed crime novel with the stunning surprise ending. And once again, the seemingly ageless writer is keeping good on her promise she made way back in 1963, in a piece she penned for The Saturday Review, her first national exposure as a writer. Regarding writing, she wrote in Confessions of an Unpublished Writer. "… I expect to practice it for as many years as I have left on earth."*

Let's take just a minute and parse that paragraph a bit and talk about why each word and/or sentence is there and why it's in the order it is written.

*Nonagenarian* **(I wanted to say right up front and declare that this is a 90-plus-year-old writer. That's interesting, even before you know anything else. It's remarkable, and it's a great hook for freelance writers and reporters who are always looking for an interesting angle. So, it's in the first sentence, and is even the very first word on the first page of the press kit.)** *novelist Babette Hughes has done it again.* **(I wanted the reader to know that she is not a first time novelist, a rank amateur who is just now getting started with her writing career. She has done it…*again.* That confirms that she has done it before, right?)**

*She has penned a powerful follow-up to The Hat, award-winning acclaimed crime novel with the stunning surprise ending.* **(I'm suggesting to anyone reading this that if they like the story we are about to describe, and if they are intrigued at all, they should run right out and get a copy of the first novel. Or, they should ask me to send them one, which, of course, I'd be happy to do.)**

*And once again, the seemingly ageless writer is keeping good on her promise she made way back in 1963, in a piece she penned for The Saturday Review, her first national exposure as a writer.* **(This is to establish a pedigree. You don't get published in *The Saturday Review* unless you're really, really good.)**

*Regarding writing, she wrote in Confessions of an Unpublished Writer. "… I expect to practice it for as many years as I have left on earth."* **( An emotional hook,** that I hope makes the reader care enough to read the next paragraph of the executive summary)

After the executive summary, we have the bio and a picture. Hopefully we have intrigued you in the exec summary about this this writer, so let us now tell you a bit more about her.

## About Babette Hughes

In her first published work, a national article penned back in 1963, for *The Saturday Review* titled *Confessions of an Unpublished Writer,* Babette Hughes wrote these words that turned out to be more than a little prophetic:

*It (writing) is no easy calling, but its rewards go so far beyond the mundane that I expect to practice it for as many years as I have left on this earth.*

Almost half a century later she is keeping her word, publishing her second novel next month while also writing a third for future publication. *The Red Scarf,* a much anticipated follow-up to her award-winning novel, *The Hat,* will publish in June of 2013.

Born in Cleveland Ohio, Babette grew up in the time of Prohibition and bootleggers. Her father was one of the first bootleggers in the country, and was murdered by the mafia in a turf war at the age of 29. Babette's mother, a tragic figure even before the death of her husband, sank into damage and denial, telling Babette that her father had died of an incurable disease.

But, at age 12, her older brother revealed the unvarnished truth about their father and he even sent her to the public library to read the archived copies of *The Plain Dealer* for herself, with all the gory and troubling details.

"I look back at all of that now," she says, "and I must have been pretty brave to go and read for myself about it, learn all of that, and then to keep it to myself for all those years."

Writing has allowed her to draw from those unusual life experiences to create her characters and tell their stories (and sometimes cautionary tales) in vivid detail. Gangsters and guns, women and wine, sin and society all melded together in riveting detail for readers from all walks of life who somehow relate to the characters she creates. She explains that phenomenon by saying, "I find that the personal is universal, if you take the time to tell the story right. Though these stories are loosely based on real characters I have known and my own experiences, I find it gratifying, but not surprising, really, when readers tell me that they identify with them and their plight."

Now 90, she still writes every day with a fluidity and grace of a woman half her age. Why does she keep writing?

"The truth is liberating, but sometimes elusive." She explains, "I'm always looking for it and how to best write about it, and I probably always will."

She is married to JD Hughes and lives in Austin, Texas. They are the parents and step-parents of eight children.

## Alex Charfen

Alex Charfen has an inspiring story.

Period.

He and his wife Cadey lost everything a few years ago in the Florida real estate bust, but instead of quitting, they got back into the game here in Austin, Texas, and they changed the way they did business from the ground up.

What they did, worked. They hit #23 on the *Inc.* magazine list of America's fastest growing companies just a couple of years ago, and the growth of their company is still practically straight up.

The whole thing is remarkable. Along the way, Alex, a voracious reader and learner, has become a top speaker and a business expert who sees things differently.

In this bio that we wrote for him, I wanted to stress that he had developed a concept that he built a business on. The concept is *congruency*, Intrigued? I hope so.

I wanted to tell his and Cadey's comeback story because I knew that there were a lot of people riding out a rough economy who could use the encouragement.

# Alex Charfen

Alex Charfen—entrepreneur, teacher, author, speaker—is on a mission. Though not yet 40 years old, he has spent three decades on the front lines of entrepreneurialism and business. His journey has taught him many things, but he believes he has discovered one key that could change everything for small business owners.

"I think everyone knows in their heart that they have to align their business with their personal values," he says. "But the big question is *how?* How do you do that? It sounds simple, but getting there is the hard part. I've learned that there are very specific steps."

He calls the concept *congruency*, and his ideas are starting a revolution.

Born in Mexico City, but raised in California by an entrepreneurial father and school teacher mom, Alex learned early on about the opportunities and perils of small business. His father opened a factory to produce interlocking concrete roofing tiles to take advantage of the California housing boom of the '70s. But soon the end of the '70s brought a downturn, and with it, a dramatic change in the Charfen fortunes.

"I learned right then and there that we all do what we have to do," says Alex.

In many ways, Alex followed in his father's footsteps. He and wife Cadey invested heavily in the Florida real estate boom of the late '90s, and soon found themselves prosperous but highly leveraged. When the market took a dive, they lost everything and were forced to declare bankruptcy.

"It was," says Alex, "my darkest hour."

Ever the student, Alex took away many nuggets from that experience and, like his father before him, began to rebuild, albeit with fundamental changes this time. He found natural allies among real estate agents who were also suffering around the country, and who had little idea what to do with the growing multitude of homes in foreclosure. He and Cadey launched the Distressed Property Institute, and began to teach other real estate professionals what they had learned, offering them education, tools, and hope. They also found that many of these principles applied to any small business, and The Charfen Institute was formed. In four short years it has become one of the fastest growing small businesses in the country.

Alex has worked tirelessly, made smart decisions, found great team members, and prospered personally and professionally, with *congruency* as the centerpiece of his business and life. His mantra is simple: "I wake up every day determined to be the best husband I can be, the best father I can be, and to help as many people as possible achieve their goals. I have found a way to build my business *with* these values, not in spite of them. And I've learned that when small business owners really do this, long-term success is practically guaranteed."

Alex and Cadey live in Austin, Texas, and have two daughters, Kennedy and Reagan.

# Communicating at the Speed of Light

For most of our history, humans have communicated at the speed of sound. We started out talking to each other and then, we invented phones and we started calling each other. Then—just a very a few years ago, really—we began to communicate electronically with email and texts. It was so easy! No stamps to lick, no envelopes to fill out, no hunting around for stationary and a good pen. You could just sit down and write your friend a note and punch "send," and off it went.

What a wonderful development but, I would say, one loaded with unseen danger.

Think for a minute about how that transformed how we do what we do every day. In the publicity business, for example, you used to have to put packets together and send them out in the mail. That involved writing and printing press kits, having someone stuff envelopes with books and papers. Then, you had to go down to an actual post office and stand in line and mail them out, hoping that they wouldn't somehow be lost in the mail or in the mailroom at their respective destinations. In those days, the book reviewers at the big media outlets were getting hundreds of those packets *every week*. What were the chances that they would sift through that mountain of mail and open your package? Slim, or none—unless there were powerful forces at work to make them do so.

Now, I pull a list of media contacts, sometimes as many as 300 to 400. I write a press kit and an email pitch, and then I start sending them out immediately. I can send 100 or more of those every single day via email. And, if I do a good job and write the right words to grab their attention, I get an immediate response.

So, how can communicating at the speed of light not be a great thing? In fact, it *is* a great thing with these two caveats:

- **It's easy, so everybody is doing it**—Remember my CNBC contact? She gets 800 emails a day. That's too many to read.

- **It's immediate**—The good news? We can pop a message out to people at the speed of light. The bad news? We can pop a message out to people at the speed of light. It's easier than ever to make bonehead mistakes when we rush, and now the whole system is built for breakneck speed.

Have you ever sent an email out in a hurry and wanted to immediately draw it back to yourself because you realized that you had misspoken? We've probably all done it at one time or another, at least the sensitive communicators among us. The insensitive communicators apparently have no idea that they are crushing you with words, so they don't think about recalling messages very often. I had a boss once, a kind and gentle person for the most part, but her emails were entirely too blunt and curt. Interestingly, she had no idea that they were like that until I replied to one of her messages and she had to read the whole email string to get the gist of the note. To her credit, she was appalled by what she had written. From then on she became a much more sensitive communicator in all aspects.

> If we're going to be effective communicators, we have to take our time and get *every* message as right is can be. When we're emotional or rattled, we shouldn't send messages out, especially to people we don't know.

If we're going to be effective communicators, we have to take our time and get *every* message as right is can be. When we're emotional or rattled, we shouldn't send messages out, especially to people we don't know.

Recently, I had what could have been a very testy email exchange with a new media contact that I had never met and with whom I had never had any previous correspondence. What ultimately happened in this exchange is what you hope happens in these moments. It is the greatest turnaround I have ever had, and yet it was fraught with disaster; there were at least a couple of times in the exchange where I could have fired back immediately and it would have nuked the relationship and any possibility of getting coverage for my client's book.

It began with this initial note written to someone we'll call "Walter," and this note had a copy of the press kit attached. The bold type in the email message is my commentary and observation.

## The "Walter" Turnaround

*Good afternoon, Walter. I hope you've had a great week so far.* (**Always greet people and be gracious, even if they are a total stranger. It matters. Trust me.**)

*Let me begin by saying that, as a rule, I do not usually do publicity on novels, but I read this one and quite frankly couldn't put it down.* (**This was me anticipating that there might be some pushback because the book is published by a vanity press.**) *Relic of Darkness is the second novel for Austin author James S. Parker, and I found it to be mysterious, riveting, and thoroughly enjoyable. It will publish in February.*

*I have always been a huge Hitchcock fan, and this story reminded me often of his work. The James MacBridan character is an interesting protagonist, flawed and yet brave and unrelenting. The gloomy and overcast Scottish Highlands provide the backdrop to a story that has many twists and turn and surprises.*

*I've attached pdf of the book and a press kit with a brief overview of the book and a Q&A with the author.*

*I hope you can cover it.*

*Thanks in advance for your time and consideration.* (**Once again, always thank people and be gracious.**)

So, that was my initial note to the book reviews editor at this magazine that specializes in suspense novels and crime stories. Note that it's short, and to the point, and its intention is not to tell everything I know about the book and/or the author. The intent here is to pique the reader's interest enough to cause them to at least open up the press kit and read it, even if they will never read the book (highly likely).

When you do what I do all day every day, this is the most suspenseful part of the job. You send off a note like this and you hope to hear something back. Most often, in my business, people do *not* reply. But, frankly, we don't need all of them to get excited about your book or idea, we just need some of them to do so, and then we can start building momentum.

After a brief period here's the reply that I received from Walter:

*I did a quick search on Amazon and it doesn't even come up. Who is the publisher?*

Okay. This is trouble. The conversation is just about to end before it even starts. It is likely that they do not do anything with self-published novels, and, if so, we are dead in the water here. I had to think quick....

*Hi Walter.*

*It's being published by Tate. Here's a link to their site:*

*http://www.tatepublishing.com/*

*They haven't gone live with the book's website, but that should be very soon since the book publishes next month.*

*If you should need anything else from me, please do not hesitate to ask.*

*Thanks!*

So, this response is meant to take him off the trail a bit. Yes, it's published by Tate. Yes, they are a vanity publisher which he will figure out in short order. But there's legitimacy here: a website with the book on it. In fact, it's not just *a* website, it's *the publisher's* website. Then, I add a comment about the book's website to bolster my claim of legitimacy here. Finally, a friendly closing asking if he needs anything else from me.

We can't be defensive here in this exchange. After all, their policy (however dated) is their policy and I don't want to offend this editor or cast aspersions on their antiquated ideas about self-published books, so I tried to be gracious and professional.

But then, this:

*Dennis,*

*Tate is a vanity press, meaning the authors pay to be published, meaning they are self-published. I'm afraid we don't review self-published books.*

That sound you hear is the sound of all of the air going out of our campaign, at least with this outlet and its closed-minded representative. It sounds to the untrained ear like we are finished with our conversation and I and my author have lost the argument, yes?

So, what did I do? Well, I got completely aggravated and did what we all do from time to time. I sat down and banged away angrily and wrote a really scathing reply telling him that this is 2013, and by golly there are a lot of *big* self-published books out there, and who did he think he was telling *me* what's legitimate? And so on and so on....

But then, I did something most of us don't do and it saved my bacon. I did *not* send the message and instead I archived it for the night.

This was a really, really good idea.

The next morning, I woke up and pulled the note up and read it and was appalled at what I had penned in my moment of self-righteous anger. I sat down at my keyboard and tried again, this time thinking through every word and every line (again, the bold type in the message is my commentary):

> Then, I did something most of us don't do and it saved my bacon. I did *not* send the message and instead I archived it for the night. This was a really, really good idea.

*You know, Walter, I normally don't take books that are self-published* (**Now, I am agreeing with him. Common ground is established immediately, and his defenses are probably down. Just think how many ugly responses he gets to his "we don't do self-published books" philosophy. And yet, instead of an ugly response, he is actually getting agreement**), *but this year I have taken a chance on a couple and had tremendous results, mainly because the books are really good* (**That's an un-offensive way of making my point that in all of the self-published crap out there, there are good books, and I should know that because this is what I do; and by the way, it's also what you do and you should know this, too**).

(**Now, I am moving in the for the kill**) *I just finished a campaign with a self-published author who wound up being featured on CNBC.com. and Forbes, and became a regular contributor to The Huff Post and Psychology Today.* (**I'm still not saying I'm right or that he's wrong, I'm just making the point by using a real-life example to buttress my previous point that there are some good ones in the lot. This also says that other, more influential publications agree with me and have shined their spotlights on a self-published book. The unasked question here is "why aren't you guys following these very smart and influential people who really don't care who published it as long as it's good?"**)

*It seems like the worm is turning (ever so slightly) on the credibility of (some) self-published books.* (**See, I am *still* agreeing with him here, in a way, even after not so gently shooting down his theory about self-published books.**) *As you know, most of them are not very good, but occasionally there is a diamond in the rough like this one.* (**Translation: I know what I'm talking about and I wouldn't send you something that was not worth your while—keeping in mind my earlier point that I did this same thing with another self-published book that did well with the media. I've done this before, and I'm telling you this one *is* different.**)

*Thanks for taking the time to respond. I appreciate it greatly.* (**Closing with a gracious close. And, the fact is, I *do* appreciate him taking the time to go back and forth like this. He's a magazine editor and probably**

**has other things to do. Instead, he's conversing with me. That's very kind of him.)**

*Have a good weekend.*

*Dennis*

Now, for the payoff from Walter:

*Dennis,*

*While we don't review self-published books* **(Okay. I think we've established that. But, wait. There's more. Get ready: he's about to change his mind completely!)**, *we do have some of the authors do guest posts on our site which get a pretty nice amount of traffic.* **(Cue the Heavenly music!)** *We do a couple features on a regular basis, Behind the books, which is kind of a DVD extra telling the tale behind the book, five movies/ or books/ or albums that changed my life (self-explanatory) and also pet spotlights, where authors talk about their pets. Each is a chance for the author to let people get to know them and then they can also pimp the book a bit at the end. If Mr. Parker* **(Now my author is Mr. Parker! He didn't matter at all just two or three little emails ago, and now he's Mr. Parker?)** *had an interest in doing one of these, we'd be glad to run it and buzz it on social media.*

And there you have it. A complete one-eighty, all because I didn't respond with my gut and just fire off a note giving him a piece of my mind. As you may have figured out by now, I'm very passionate about the people and books I work on and that would have been by far the easiest response. I might have even felt good for just a minute. But then, it would have been horrible for my author, it would have wrecked my relationship with this fellow, and kept me from pitching future books to him; and most importantly, it would have just plain been the wrong thing to do.

## Cosmetics and Spacing

It's never too late to learn something new. A while back I tried a little experiment that yielded some interesting results. I was doing outreach on Roger Wright's book *Finding Work When There Are No Jobs*, and this was my first foray:

---

Good afternoon, _____ I hope your New Year is off to a running start.

I am working on a terrific new book by Roger Wright, an author who I first met when we both worked at The Gallup Organization. It's called *Finding Work When There Are No Jobs*. I've always believed that Roger was Gallup's best writer, and we've stayed in pretty close touch over the years after we had both left the company. A while back he called me and said he had written a book on jobs, and my first thought was, "Oh, no. Another one of those books that tell you what levers to pull to find work. That's only been written about a thousand times." But then, he sent the manuscript to me and I absolutely fell in love with it. It's filled with powerful stories, not formulas, and it is written to take the reader on *their* journey (not his) to finding meaningful work that they are born to do.

The stories are centered around "The Five," five organizing principles. They are:

- **Tell Your Story**—and that doesn't mean writing a good resume. Resumes are necessary to outline your work history and list your skills, but the greatest resume in the world can't tell people *who you are.*

- **Add Music**—Use the elements of music—rhythm, harmony, and melody to prompt new ways of thinking about how to differentiate yourself from the rest of the world.

- **Communitize**—Stop networking. Start communitizing. Weave yourself into the fabric of every community you can. You'll find out where you can fill a need from the inside, as a community member. Not as a networker.

- **Solve a Mystery**—What is it that you can do with such ease that others see as a mystery? Mysteries always indicate a need for a solution. What if you could fill that need, solve what appears to be a mystery to others—and get paid for it?

- **Practice Stewardship**—Take care of something bigger than you. Find a way to build a legacy in real time.

Then, he has action items around each, practical to-dos to help the reader arrive at a plan that works for them, so they can go forward with confidence at a time that can be confidence-sapping.

*Finding Work* publishes February 4, 2013.

Any interest?

Dennis

---

Thud.

I got hardly any response at all, and I felt like this was a pretty good pitch for the book.

I couldn't understand it.

Then, it hit me. People are too busy to read a lot of "gray," and maybe their lack of interest had nothing to do with the content, but something to do with the way the content looked on the page.

My first thought after coming up with this gem? *Crazy!*

But, I decided that it was worth a try. So, I re-sent the message, but on the second round, it looked like this:

---

Good afternoon, _____. I hope your New Year is off to a running start.

I am working on a terrific new book by Roger Wright, an author who I first met when we both worked at The Gallup Organization. It's called *Finding Work When There are No Jobs*.

I've always believed that Roger was Gallup's best writer, and we've stayed in pretty close touch over the years after we had both left the company.

A while back he called me and said he had written a book on jobs, and my first thought was, "Oh, no. Another one of those books that tell you what levers to pull to find work. That's only been written about a thousand times."

But then, he sent the manuscript to me and I absolutely fell in love with it. It's filled with powerful stories, not formulas, and it is written to take the reader on *their* journey (not his) to finding meaningful work that they are born to do.

The stories are centered around "The Five," five organizing principles. They are:

- **Tell Your Story**—and that doesn't mean writing a good resume. Resumes are necessary to outline your work history and list your skills, but the greatest resume in the world can't tell people *who you are*.

- **Add Music**—Use the elements of music—rhythm, harmony, and melody to prompt new ways of thinking about how to differentiate yourself from the rest of the world.

- **Communitize**—Stop networking. Start communitizing. Weave yourself into the fabric of every community you can. You'll find out where you can fill a need from the inside, as a community member. Not as a networker.

- **Solve a Mystery**—What is it that you can do with such ease that others see as a mystery? Mysteries always indicate a need for a solution. What if you could fill that need, solve what appears to be a mystery to others—and get paid for it?

- **Practice Stewardship**—Take care of something bigger than you. Find a way to build a legacy in real time.

Then, he has action items around each, practical to-dos to help the reader arrive at a plan that works for them, so they can go forward with confidence at a time that can be confidence-sapping.

*Finding Work* publishes February 4, 2013.

Any interest?

Dennis

---

Note the subtle difference here. The content is exactly the same, but the spacing is slightly different, with very subtle spacing changes. The response was immediate and strong, and we started getting media hits immediately.

The lesson here? Sometimes people see a lot of gray in a message and it appears to be too much to bear and wade through. They zone out, or give up before they get a chance to see what you're trying to say. Make it easier for them. It's okay to put complicated ideas into an email, but be careful about the cosmetics.

Remember, people are overwhelmed and busy. Important people and gatekeepers are worse off than that, if that's possible. Be their friend. Make it easy to read. They might just reward you with a meeting, or coverage, or whatever you might be looking for.

> Sometimes people see a lot of gray in a message and it appears to be too much to bear and wade through. They zone out, or give up before they get a chance to see what you're trying to say. Make it easier for them. It's okay to put complicated ideas into an email, but be careful about the cosmetics.

# Be Gracious and Polite

It seems like a no-brainer, doesn't it? It's kind of like I shouldn't even have to say it.

> A lot of people communicate like cavemen with email. I'm all for brevity, but a few niceties, especially when you are dealing with people you hardly know or have never met is really important and it only takes an extra second or two to do.

But, alas, I do. Why? Because a lot of people communicate like cavemen with email. I'm all for brevity, but a few niceties, especially when you are dealing with people you hardly know or have never met is really important and it only takes an extra second or two to do. Once you get in the habit of doing it, you won't even think about it. You'll just do it. And, all your readers who are getting horribly blunt, unfeeling emails all day will be glad you took the time to get it right.

So, it's simple. Be Polite. For example, when you send an email to somebody, greet them:

*"Good morning, Bob. I hope your week is off to a terrific start."*

And, yes, if you know something is going on with them that's important (perhaps you've even discussed it), ask about it.

*"How's the new baby?"*

*"How did your daughter's graduation go?"*

Then, get right into the body of the message and the reason you wrote the note in the first place.

At the end of your message, thank the reader.

*"I appreciate your time today, Bob."* Or, *"Thanks for taking the time to look it over, Bob."*

I have learned two things from all these years of communicating with thousands (maybe tens of thousands) of people via email through the years. One, being kind and thoughtful never gets old. We live in a culture that can be pretty crass sometimes. But, people have not changed. They really appreciate the greetings and the thank you's. Remember that many of the people you reach out to have thankless jobs, and every email that doesn't acknowledge how grateful you are for spending their time on your behalf only reinforces that.

So, be kind.

## A Word about Social Media

You'll notice that we have talked very little about social media so far. That is not meant in any way to discount the value of social media. It's vital that you have a strategy and all of the tools to participate in and speak to this powerful medium and its "followers."

But, remember that these cool new tools are just that—tools. The rules are for the most part the same as for any medium. These are conversations and they are meant to be just that—conversations.

I have mistakenly followed people on twitter who only tweet when they have a new property for sale. They never just contribute something to the conversation, How would you like it if every time you saw your friend, you said "Hello" and he or she said, "Can I show you a picture of the cool house I'm trying to sell in North Austin?" After a few times of trying to have a conversation with this person, you would give up and maybe even start avoiding them.

That happens in social media all the time.

> With social media, you have your audience in a virtual room with you, so be kind. Add something to the conversation that they'll care about. Say hello, so to speak. Respond appropriately. The cool tools are new, but the rules of the road, communication-wise, are the same.

Social media has given us all a chance to have conversations with people that we would never have been able to find 10 or 15 years ago.

We can "friend" them, follow them on Twitter, and so forth, and maybe we can even have a conversation with them.

Bottom line: With social media, you have your audience in a virtual room with you, so be kind. Add something to the conversation that they'll care about. Say hello, so to speak. Respond appropriately. The cool tools are new, but the rules of the road, communication-wise, are the same.

# A
# Thousand Words

Several years ago I wrote a memoir called *Rich People Shop Here*. It originated from a short story I had written many years before for the Sunday *Houston Chronicle*. I actually wrote three articles that they accepted and ran. One was called *Breathe*, a story about taking Lamaze classes when our first child was born. The second one was called *War in the Mailbox*, a story about how my brother used to send home reel-to-reel tapes to us when he was in Vietnam. The last one told the true story of how, when we were young, our mother would take us to second-hand stores and thrift shops to buy our school clothes. When we would pull up in front of the store and park, she would always say, "Now, don't you boys feel bad about shopping in these kinds of places, because a lot of rich people shop here." I realized as I got older that if wealth can be measured by something other than money, perhaps a good life, a great reputation, and good friends, then my mom is indeed one of the richest people I know. So, in fact, rich people *did* shop there after all. There was a tremendous response to the stories, and so I set about to write a book about our family, never really intending to publish it.

There was some interest from traditional publishers though, and eventually I had a very helpful meeting with an editor at a large publishing house in Colorado Springs. He sat me down in their conference room and started his critique of the manuscript.

His main criticism? He liked my writing, and loved the story, but the chapters were too long and "people don't read like that anymore." That was five or six years ago, and it came as a bit of a surprise to me. I took his advice and found natural breaks in my manuscript and shortened the chapters significantly. Eventually it was published and made available to the public, and it has done well.

His observation bothered me a little back then that we as people are not able to focus for long periods of time on even the simplest of stories. This was not a historic tome, or a book about something complicated, like Astronomy or Physics. It was a simple, easy-to-follow story, and it was apparently going to be too complicated for readers out there unless I shortened the chapters and put in more breaks.

Well, these days it's even worse. If CNBC or *Forbes* or *The Huffington Post* asks for a guest post, they expect it to be less than 1,000 words, as a rule. Anything over that is probably not going to be read. It's *too long*.

> If CNBC or *Forbes* or *The Huffington Post* asks for a guest post, they expect it to be less than 1,000 words, as a rule.

The same is true of most marketing letters and letters in general. Most people won't read (or at least are not interested in reading) more than a page or two at most.

So, how do you do that? How do you take a really complex idea and describe it in a way that will make me care about it in less than 1,000 words?

## Marketing Letters

Let's begin with marketing letters. Here's the temptation—you want to tell people *everything* in this letter; right? This might be your only chance. So why not just put it all in there so that you are sure that you didn't leave anything out?

When I was in college, I worked several years for a well-known Houston mattress and furniture company, owned by two really great guys. One of them was in charge of our advertising, and the lets-put-it-all-in-there philosophy reigned supreme in his mind. I mean, after all, we are paying for this space in the daily paper, it's expensive and so…

The problem with that is that if you fill all your space with everything you sell, it makes it hard for me as a potential and interested buyer to find what I'm really looking for in all the hail of ink on the page.

The same is true of marketing letters and letters in general.

So, let me just give the Five Commandments of marketing letters:

- Remember, letters and emails are meant to be conversation *starters,* not the entire conversation. And, the initial communication with potential buyers of your products or services need not require an immediate buying response.

- The more you can tailor the letter for your reader, the better the chances of starting a conversation.

- Never make it appear that you are writing a form letter. People hate those, and they don't usually respond positively.

- Brevity. Brevity. Brevity. And did I say be brief?

- Don't do faceless emails about your product and setting up meetings, etc. Again, you may feel like you are accomplishing something, but I'm here to tell you that you most certainly are *not*.

> Remember, letters and emails are meant to be conversation *starters*, not the entire conversation. And, the initial communication with potential buyers of your products or services need not require an immediate buying response.

Before I move on, let me present a shining example of the many (perhaps daily) emails I get from well-meaning business development people that are, well…not what you should be doing. My comments are in bold.

**OK. First of all there's no greeting. Not 'hello,' Not 'Dear Dennis.' Nothing. Bad form. Very impersonal and crass, in my opinion.**

*I would like to introduce myself as your new _____ account contact for New York and New Jersey.* **The blank is a technology that I have never heard of and am wholly unfamiliar with. I don't need an account contact for something that I don't understand and am not currently using.**

*Let's schedule 15-20 minutes to talk about how you can best utilize our private cloud and Infrastructure-as-a-Service solution, _____.* **Uh…no. Let's not.**

*Just let me know the best day and time for us to speak about our solutions and how we move forward.* **Again, I don't think so.**

*I will also be in the area at the end of May and June. Select your nearest city to meet with me in person.* **If you click on the cities, not one is in Texas; I live in Austin. The closest clickable city is in Missouri. Hmmm… this might be a problem, yes?**

*I look forward to speaking with you. I can be reached at _____.*

*Thanks,*

Sadly, somebody is getting paid to send out this kind of mostly worthless attempt at marketing.

We can do better than this.

## Guest Blogs and Articles

In the new world of PR and publicity, powerful online entities ask that my authors and clients write guest articles for the site's audience. This seems like the perfect scenario in my opinion. If we send a book off to be reviewed, there's a 50/50 chance that the review will be negative. But, if we write a guest article, we get to frame the conversation.

Here's another positive—if we are asked to serialize over a set period of time, we can let the line out as slow or fast as we choose, yes? In other words, if I am a regular contributor to the *Huffington Post,* I don't have to cram everything I know into one article. We can gently start and continue a conversation because we have a large stage and the luxury of time. If we are granted only one article with no promise of another, then we have to press a little and make sure we get as many of our critical messages in as possible.

> If we send a book off to be reviewed, there's a 50/50 chance that the review will be negative. But, if we write a guest article, we get to frame the conversation.

The good news is that this is a lot of fun, and the challenge of getting it right is what wakes me up every day excited about my job.

Let's take a look a few successful guest blogs with a little back story on each.

This first one was written primarily to showcase the fact that my clients were experts in their field. The group I was working with was and still is considered to be experts in the healthcare business and how to make the delivery of healthcare more efficient.

It occurred to me that it would be helpful if they had a prominent doctor that they had worked with who had seen success with their ideas write a guest blog that praises them without sounding like a sales brochure for their consulting services.

In this case, Dr. Haro was kind enough to let me interview him and help him write this piece for *The Huffington Post*. I basically did this one the way I do bios. I interviewed Dr. Haro, transcribed the interview by hand, then wrote a first draft for him to work from.

My commentary is in bold.

# Patients First
By Dr. Luis Haro, M.D.

---

Somewhere, out in the highways and byways, beyond all the political wrangling and hand-wringing about health care, there is a steady stream of real people with real maladies who are entering emergency departments hoping to see a doctor for help. Night and day they come, literally by the thousands. Some leave without ever being seen. Some languish for hours in hallway beds awaiting care. Some die while they wait. **(This opening paragraph was meant to say succinctly that we have a problem. It was also written to create some tension and emotion about the issue and connect the reader right away to the problem that needs to be solved and why they should care about it).**

This is heartbreaking, and completely fixable. It's not easy, but it is doable. I've done it twice and I've seen the impact that investing a few hours and really studying every aspect of healthcare delivery can have on patient care, costs, efficiency, and overall satisfaction. **(This establishes credibility and says not only has the author been there, he's had a hand in actually fixing these problems. He's not proposing all of this in theory.)**

When I arrived at the Mayo Clinic in Rochester in 2000, I was focused on education and research. In year three, I was asked to chair the Quality Committee of the Emergency Department. It was a Mayo Clinic requirement that every committee have a physician leader. By the second meeting (maybe even halfway through the first meeting) I realized that I was not familiar with the language being used; it was engineering and practice terms that I was wholly unfamiliar with. Typically, clinicians will seek more rooms and more staff. Our main issue was to make better use of the facilities we already had, and figure out how to cut wait times for patients and increase efficiency in every way possible with our current resources.

I sought out and found a quality mentor on the Mayo staff and they helped me begin to grasp the taxonomy and the scope of the task ahead of us. I studied process improvement and cultural change. I had a great team, and we began to eliminate redundancy and wait time. We reduced unnecessary steps in the process and soon began to experience amazing results. Over time, we continued to improve, and the patients were the beneficiaries.

But soon, our improvement leveled off, and we started thinking about what else we could do. One day, one of our staff said, "You know, other industries have figured out how to take every step out of the process that doesn't add value. Why can't we do that?" We reached outside of the Mayo Clinic for help and found a new partner, this time a Lean consultant who helped us begin to understand the value streams, and the process itself.

Over the next two years, we learned to create flow in our emergency department, our staff was engaged and happier, and there was no hallway care at all.

All of this happened because the Mayo Clinic understood that adding more staff and more rooms was not the solution to their problem. You have to eliminate waste before you decide to invest in more people and more space, or you only expand the systemic inefficiency problem to a bigger canvas.

It took a while, but after a couple of years on the Quality Committee it occurred to me: In healthcare, *doctors* are trained to detect disease and fix it; *nurses* are trained to deliver health care, to give medication, take vital signs, assist the patient with their personal needs, and so on; *administrators* are trained to manage human resources and to strategically deploy capital.

But *nobody* in health care is trained to reduce waste and perfect processes. Interestingly clinicians *do* something like continuous improvement in other areas that we work in, especially research into the things that are killing us. That's why the mortality rates are better these days than they were 30 years ago, and cures for diseases and new discoveries are being found. But, the gift for making the system itself more efficient for the patient is *not* a part of what doctors do every day, nor is it anywhere in the training we receive and frankly, it should be.

## On to Texas

After leaving Mayo, I became the Medical Director at Trinity Mother Francis Hospital in Tyler, Texas, a sprawling, very busy Emergency Department with 14 overworked emergency doctors, and 64,000 annual patients (in a facility where 52,000 was capacity). What I learned very quickly when we started the process improvement was that this was already a tremendous team of people who were doing amazing work, but knew they could do more and be much more efficient. On Friday and Saturday nights, the hallways would fill up with beds because the emergency room was doing its usual land office business, and our systems were, if not broken, at least cracked and in need of a fundamental change.

Here's what happened. We replicated what we did at Mayo, and even though the number of patients we see has grown, we have become more efficient at delivering care to each and every one of them without adding any physical space. **(This section about making these changes in Texas was written to say that this template can work in any setting where the hospital is committed to it.)**

How did we do this? Well, first of all we reminded ourselves that the patient is *the* focus of our work. Anything that doesn't add value to the patient experience was dropped or changed so that it would add value. As doctors, we had to realize that the process was *not* about us, and we had to subjugate what we thought worked best for us to what worked best for the patient. Period.

The good news? This can be replicated at any hospital at any time in any part of the country. It will require a paradigm shift, and it will mean that doctors will have to spend some time in meetings and heading up committees that need their contributions. But, I've been there and I can tell you that the short-term investment is worth it. I got into the healthcare field to save lives, and the last thing I planned on doing was to chair a committee and study process improvement. In the beginning, I asked myself how all of that ancillary activity could have anything to do with my mission and calling. **(This ties all of the work to his calling and the calling of readers who may be in the medical field.)**

But, I've seen the answer to that question firsthand, and I continue to see it each and every day. The bottom line is this for those of us in the healthcare field: The process should be designed for one thing and one thing only—to serve the patient. And, when you actually do that, the results are stunning.

---

*Dr. Luis Haro is Medical Director at Trinity Mother Frances Hospital in Tyler, Texas (http://www.tmfhs.org/MotherFrancesHospitalTyler).*

This next article was written by Karl Ohaus, and was meant to be the follow up to Dr. Haro's article. Karl has worked extensively with Dr.

Haro through the years and is certainly qualified to talk about their work together.

Again, we made this article happen in roughly the same way. I interviewed Karl by phone. Then, I transcribed the interview and wrote a first draft for him to start from.

## Patients First—Part 2
By Karl Ohaus

Just last week in this space, Dr. Luis Haro talked about the stunning results that can be achieved when you put patients first. **(The idea of course is to drive readers back to the first piece).** The idea of focusing every person involved and every part of the process on one thing seems revolutionary and, at first glance, near impossible with all the day-to-day distractions. Have you ever been in a big city emergency department on a Friday or Saturday night? It seems like complete chaos; and yet, when it's done right, it can be a beautiful dance that fulfills the primary mission of most healthcare professionals that I know: saving lives and healing people.

In many places across the country, that mission is in deep trouble. While healthcare is full of very talented and dedicated people, they are working extremely hard in systems that are, quite frankly, completely broken. Even worse, these wildly talented people are not being effectively used to fix the problems.

Where do you start? First, I would set the bar high for what could be. Make bold statements about what you would like to see happen for the hurting people who show up in your healthcare facility, and then figure out how to get there. For example, you could say that "No one should leave an ER department without being seen." That happens a lot these days and, as you may have read in Dr. Haro's article last week, it can be rectified with the right organizational medicine and a commitment to the process. But, like any *big fix*, it begins with an honest assessment of the problems. Be honest about your issues, but set the bar high for your outcomes.

I would suggest that the assessment of your current situation be done by and with those talented people on your team who are scurrying from one crisis to another. I'd assemble a team that has people from each of the silos that affect the patient experience, and start by asking:

- Do we agree on our purpose as a team?
- Who is our customer?
- Why do they come?
- What do they expect when they get here?

Then, I would ask them to define the high-level process steps in the patient journey:

- Does it start at triage, when the patient walks through the door, or when the ambulance makes contact?
- Where and when are patients waiting?
- When is our team waiting?

By the way, the "When is our team waiting?" question is important and often overlooked. I learned a lot from an experience I had spending two days with a team just observing their emergency department. We gleaned a great deal by simply watching the process from start to finish and seeing as an outsider where the process breaks down or lags or—even worse—fails completely.

Most ER doctors and administrators believe they are too busy every day putting out fires and problem solving to do such a thing, but I can tell you that just spending some time and objectively watching the comings and goings will go a long way toward starting to solve the problems. Spend some time observing and you may find that you have fewer fires to put out going forward. That seems like a good long-term investment, doesn't it? In fact, one healthcare institution took it even a step further. The department chair stayed with a patient from the time they walked thru the door to the time they were discharged, and this exercise led to an epiphany that changed their processes for the better.

Next, I would define the problems that need to be solved:

- If our purpose is to treat patients, why do we have patients who leave without being seen?

- Why if our average patient value-added time is less than 40 minutes, is our length of stay over 200 minutes?

- Why do we need to treat patients in the hallways?

- Why do our doctors spend more time filling out paperwork and on computers than they do with the patient?

The good news is that this transformational process is beginning to get a foothold in healthcare facilities around the country and around the globe. I've been privileged to see it firsthand and I've been involved in transformations that forever changed the way healthcare is delivered, and the patients and healthcare professionals have been the beneficiaries.

---

*Karl Ohaus has worked with Dr. Haro since 2008 and is one of the authors of Perfecting Patient Journeys* http://www.lean-transform.com/index.html.

This next article about Dell was proposed by my client, the CEO of Entelligence, Steve Satterwhite. At the time he suggested this article, there was a lot of news every day about Dell going private, what led up to it, and what the ramifications might be.

Steve suggested an article that talked about Entelligence's past business relationship with Dell, and why they ended it several years ago.

My suggestion was that it not be a kick-you-while-you're-down article, or sour grapes. Steve is not that kind of guy anyway, and he agreed whole-heartedly. I think we accomplished that here together.

You'll note that this breaks the 1,000-word barrier by almost double, and that was ok in this instance. It was *very* timely, and the editor at *Forbes* let it go this time. That's pretty rare, but it does happen on occasion if all the stars are lined up just right.

I also want to point out that this article ran in *Forbes* under a different title (*Forbes* chose a more provocative one—*Dell's Poisonous Culture is Sinking its Ship—And Raises Questions for Potential Buyers*).

At last count, over 21,000 people had read the article.

## Our Two Best Days with Dell

Lessons learned from days with Dell and a few questions its potential suitors may want to ask

By Stephen R. Satterwhite, Chairman & CEO – Entelligence IT

---

There's an old adage that says the two best days of owning a boat are the day you buy it and the day you sell it. I felt that way when I owned my own boat in the 1980s.

Some twenty-plus years later, I felt that same way about our client, Dell. Here's what I mean.

In the summer of 2001, our small IT services company landed on the *Inc.* 500 list (#320) as one of the fastest growing, privately-held small businesses in America. But then, a few months later, things started to unravel fast.

First, our largest client, Compaq was acquired by HP. Our work there came to a grinding halt. A few weeks after that, our country suffered the 9/11 terrorists attacks. It rocked our nation and our economy, including one of our other large clients, Continental Airlines (now United).

Then, just a few weeks later, down the street, Enron collapsed, dragging with it the companies who were also in the energy trading business—those companies that also happened to be our clients.

Thus, in a few short months, in the fall of 2001, we had lost about 60percent of our revenues. Things were looking bleak for our small company. We needed a lifeline if we were going to survive.

That lifeline appeared in the spring of 2002. We got lucky. It was simply a case of being in the right place at the right time.

And that place happened to be in middle of the sea of cubicles on the second floor of Building 2 on the Dell campus in Texas. I was there for a sales meeting that one of our account managers set up for the two of us.

At that time, Dell was looking for IT services partners to design, deploy, and configure their enterprise storage systems. We wanted to be one of those partners.

The Dell manager told us they had a "Be-Back" problem. Be-Backs was code for what he called an IT project failure, escalation, or revisit — something that goes wrong before, during, or after an IT services project.

Think Jim Carey in movie *The Cable Guy*. It sounds like this: "Hey IT consultant. The work you did today wasn't correct and the systems aren't working. So, I need you to *Be Back* out there tomorrow and fix it." Or something like that.

But, in order to win the business, they told us upfront they expected us to do three things: first, we had to be the lowest cost provider or we didn't have a shot. Second, we had to deliver the best customer service—a Very Satisfied Customer Experience—a "10" out of 10. Third, we could never, ever, ever make a mistake (i.e. a Be-Back) or we'd be gone.

Now, what I learned in business school and being an entrepreneur is that most companies are only good at one or two of those things. Not all three. But, we needed the business and we had to figure out how to do all three of these things at once.

Like most entrepreneurs, I have always been a blind optimist. Fire-Ready-Aim. I believe we can do almost anything, right? So, "no problem," I said. We can do this.

And, just like the first day when I owned my boat, when we won the contract, it was a great day for our company. We celebrated and then set out to build the business, build our relationship with them, and build the talented team to pull it all off.

Indeed, we did, with flying colors. In fact, over the next few years, our customer satisfaction scores were consistently off the charts. We figured out how to deliver services at a very low cost. And we hardly ever made a mistake. And when we did, we fixed it.

Yes, Dell demanded a lot from us and their other partners. But the good news is that we did well under that pressure and, in fact, thrived. We devised and implemented new systems that we still use today to build and maintain flawless customer relationships with no Be-Backs or complaints. As a result, we built a fairly large business for ourselves at Dell.

We did so well that, in 2005, we were named *Dell Supplier of the Year* and handed a big trophy by the CEO. For that, I am grateful.

But then, after a few years, something changed. One of the groups we were working with had a management change. They brought in two young managers who didn't know a lot about IT services. But they knew a lot about the Dell low-cost model. And almost immediately, the culture changed for the worse.

No longer were we collaborating with our customer. Instead, it became a one-way, heavy-handed culture of fear and intimidation. Their mantra was cut, cut, cut... then cut some more. But you can't cut your way to success. They didn't know that then. Maybe this is part of their woes now?

But worst of all, it was the way they treated our people that really got to me and my business partner. One day, we had enough. As I sat in one of those quarterly business reviews and watched and listened to the way the Dell team treated my team, I had finally had my fill.

You see, in our company, we have an "employees come first" culture. We subscribe to the model that, in order for us to deliver great customer service for you, we first have to deliver great employee service for our team. It's not just something that sounds good when you read the company values, it's who we are.

So, when a customer treats our people poorly, as in the case with Dell, we're no longer meeting that commitment to our employees. We're out of integrity with that value system. And, as a result, we started to lose some really great people who no longer wanted to work on the Dell account.

Over time, we realized that this culture at Dell was more systemic than just a handful of managers. In fact, I once got an email from a Dell executive warning me that they have run off or killed off a lot of other partners like us. That he liked us and said to be careful. We took that seriously and started to wake up.

We saw that it wasn't just how they treated their partners. They treated each other the same way. And Dell insiders say that in the annual employee survey, over half of the employees say they would leave for greener pastures if given the chance.

In the science of employee engagement, that means that over half of their workforce is most likely not engaged. Perhaps they've already quit the company, but they're still there drawing a paycheck?

This culture proved to be pervasive throughout every group we worked with at Dell. And it didn't look like it was going to get better, no matter how well we performed.

And so we made the hard decision to fire what had then become our biggest customer. We decided to walk away from millions of dollars a year in revenue because, well, it was the right thing to do.

The next day, I called a staff meeting for first thing in the morning. Everybody showed up. I said, in essence, "We're firing Dell. We are no longer culturally aligned."

And just like the second best day of owning my boat, I felt relieved. To my surprise, there were no gasps of air. There was no handwringing or despair over it. In fact I looked around the room and I saw a few faint smiles and even a little release on the faces of our people.

Then one of our managers said to me, "Well, if you look around this table, no one here is going to shed a tear about that. So, what's next boss?"

Now, if all this seems like sour grapes, it's not. I'm a big boy. I'm certainly not a victim. And I'm certainly no Taylor Swift of the corporate world writing about my corporate breakups.

But this is more a reflection of my own naiveté and then growth as an entrepreneur. For many years, I was blinded by the revenue and the so-called prestige that came with doing business at Dell. It kept me from making the right decisions for my people and our company.

There's another adage that says, "When one door is closed, another one is opened." For us, we were able to take what we learned from Dell and parlay it into a thriving and profitable business with customers that we were more culturally aligned with.

Now, today, I'm reading this big ship that used to rule the low-cost PC world is being taken private. And I've been reading about the potential bidding war for Dell between Silver Lake Partners, Blackstone Group, LP, and Carl Icahn.

I started thinking a lot about what this means to their company, employees, and customers, and to the IT industry as a whole. Maybe there are some lessons learned that these potential suitors should investigate. Maybe there are some hard questions these folks should be asking.

For example, some have argued all along that the low-cost model that Dell cut its teeth on is not sustainable—that sooner or later, someone will figure out how to match or even beat your costs. And that's what happened to Dell.

Dell's competitors caught up to its low-cost model. Without a significant cost advantage, it now appears to have become just another player in a highly competitive and highly commoditized IT market.

What we do know is that when companies compete in this type of environment, it's only the companies who deliver great customer service that will eventually win.

But we also know that to deliver great service, it all starts with how you treat your employees and your business partners. That's where I believe Dell will continue to struggle, unless whoever winds up owning and running the company changes it.

If I were a current Dell board member or one of the groups now engaged in a bidding war for the company, I'd ask some hard questions about the company culture. How will our culture change once the dust has cleared? How will we treat our employees and partners? What can we do to improve employee engagement?

After all, new ownership with the same culture is like putting lipstick on a pig.

I hope whatever happens with Dell, that they'll start working on their culture first. I still have a lot of friends and colleagues that work there that I care about. And we lost a lot of great people that we put on the Dell team that I wish were still here.

They deserve better.

---

*Stephen R. Satterwhite is Chairman and CEO of Entelligence IT, a fast growing data storage consulting company. This article is an excerpt from his forthcoming book. You can connect with Steve at steves@entelligence.com.*

## Your One Goal: Readers by the Throngs

All these pieces did really well. They attracted a ton of readers and got people talking. I don't want to sound cynical at all, but keep in mind what the final destination is here for the website who allows you to contribute. They want eyeballs on the site, period. Yes, they may be trying to change the world somehow, and yes, they may have a stated mission of some kind, but here's the deal—if they don't attract a ton of attention to their site they cannot sell advertising or stay in business to fight another day. So, they are expecting you to write something provocative and interesting for their readers, and they want you to share it on social media and bring a throng of readers to their site.

So, how do you do that? Well, first it's really important to remember how most people read these days. As we have established, there is entirely too much information out there. Tens of thousands of versions of stories, all shiny and flitting by, craving your attention. Some are shinier than others. Some are just fluff and others have real substance. 'Twas always thus.

Begin your piece with a provocative and interesting title. Be reasonable here. Don't just put something up there, like a spammer does when you get those goofy emails that you immediately discard. People are smart and savvy these days, and they have seen plenty. So, make it interesting, but be sure it applies to your piece. It can't be so far afield that the reader dives off into the body of the article and gets disappointed.

Secondly, let your article unfold from start to finish. Pull your reader in to the article from the get-go, and then roll out the story in a way that keeps them moving through it, undistracted and determined to get to the end to see where this story ends up.

And, here's another idea. When you give your bio info at the end of these pieces, make it *very easy* to contact you.

*Very easy.*

If it's too difficult, people won't jump through the hoops you have set up. Those days are over. For Steve Satterwhite, the answer was to put his actual personal email address in the bio. You know what that means, right? There are going be nutty people who write to you. It's a given. If they don't take the time to write directly to you, they will make a comment on the site itself.

I find it amazing that there are so many bazaar people out there, survivalists living in silos with a bag of beans and a rifle waiting in a three-point stance to pounce on anything they disagree with or do not understand.

And, get ready for this great revelation—often what they write in response to your article has absolutely positively *nothing* to do with what you wrote about in your piece. You write about fixing education, for example, and you get comments about Iraq, President Obama not having a birth certificate, and things like that.

So, if you're going to make it easy for people to reach you (recommended), learn to simply ignore the crazies that you will occasionally get. Because (thankfully) you will get a lot of appreciative comments from genuine people who are glad you took the time to write your piece. They'll tell you how your ideas helped them, and I guarantee that just one of those will make it all worth it.

# What's
# Your Song?

Until recently, I was pretty sure that I knew everything or most everything about communicating effectively. Then in the spring of 2012, I was caught completely off guard, and without any preparation for what I think was the single greatest lesson I have ever learned about communication. And it came from a songwriting experience, of all places.

Just think about it. A songwriter typically has three minutes to say everything. As we have already noted, the best of these artisans make it look easy and effortless, but as I was about to discover, it is anything but.

Every week, I get an email notice from the Nashville recording community called the *RowFax*. The *RowFax* is an alert to songwriters and publishers about who is recording and what kind of material they might be looking for. Sometimes they even go so far as to tell you what tempos they are looking for, or even what subject matter they're interested in.

In this case, a young couple, independent recording artists in Nashville, were looking for material, and as I recall, they were not very specific. Their query said something like "great songs." Well, no kidding. Who in the recording business is looking for *not* great songs? So, in response, I submitted a song of mine written years ago called *Worth My Time,* a ballad with an Irish feel; a sad song about a bad relationship with somebody who just keeps coming into your life and then going out. It's about an unstable lover, one who is maybe even a bit abusive.

I thought the original song was pretty good and most likely a finished work. My momma liked it. My friends liked it. In fact, the thought of ever rewriting it had never crossed my mind.

But, after submitting the song I got a long note from the singers and their team about how much they loved the song and how they thought that it could be a truly great song, but… it needed a rewrite to tell the story a bit better. They compared it to a well-known standard, and said they thought it could stand up to that great song if the rewrite worked well.

I have to say that at I had mixed emotions. At first I was a little put off, but then, I thought… wait a minute. There are some positives here. They are comparing my song's upside to a standard, a song that other writers

WHAT'S YOUR SONG?

admire for its emotional depth and musical and lyrical beauty. And, in fact, I have a good friend who actually co-wrote the song they are comparing it to. So I just simply forwarded the note to my songwriter friend and asked him a simple question:

*Should I pay any attention at all to this request to re-write my song?*

His response to my query was one of those moments in my life that I will never forget. It was a Sunday afternoon when he called from Nashville, and he kindly asked if I had a few minutes to discuss the song—a rhetorical question. Think about it. How often do you get this kind of opportunity? This is a professional communicator at the top of his game and he's about to offer me advice because I'm his friend and because he cares.

He began by saying that he had listened to the song in its current form, and he believed that these people were right on all counts. It is a terrific song as it is and he wasn't surprised that they had been drawn to it, but he believed that it could be one of *those* songs with a little work.

Then, it happened. You know how when you're watching a movie where everybody is shooting pool for fun and then somebody throws a hundred bucks on the table and suddenly one of the contestants steps away and opens up a nice leather case and takes out two halves of a beautiful pearl inlaid cue stick and starts powdering their hands. You quickly realize in that moment that they don't shoot pool like you. They get *paid* for it, and their approach is going to be completely different than we hobbyists. My conversation with this world-class songwriter was exactly like that. I suddenly felt like a rank amateur, and not because he did it on purpose. In spite of his significant accomplishments, he is one of the most humble people that I know. But, as I listened intently to his critique and suggestions, I realized that I still had a lot to learn about songwriting, even after having done it for almost 35 years.

This was his offer at the end of that stunning conversation—he would be my editor, he would help me think through the process, we would deconstruct the song, and start from ground zero to rebuild it. He compared it to coal mining and he said that over the next undetermined time period

118

(I was thinking maybe a couple of weeks, tops) he and I would be "inside the mountain," and we would study every square inch of the rock walls until we found exactly the right place to dig for musical gold.

Over the next four to six months, we spoke almost every day and my friend was diligent and creative beyond anything I had ever seen. Eventually, we finished the first two verses and the bridge and we began a several month quest to write the last verse. While writing the bridge, I got another shining example of my friend's remarkable and unflagging attention to detail. One day he called me up and he said, "You know, Dennis. The bridge uses the word 'seen' and I think that's the wrong word. When people are really troubled or angry, they sometimes talk to themselves. So, I think the word should be 'said.' Before, the bridge was:

*I've **seen** it all a thousand times before. What I would do if you walked through that door.*

*Now here you are and all that I can do is wait for your goodbye.*

As per my friend's suggestion, we changed that opening line to *I've **said** it all a thousand times before* and it helped the bridge to be so much more descriptive of this person in this troubled relationship with a lover who keeps coming into and going out of his or her life.

One word made that much difference?

Yes.

But we weren't nearly done just yet. It seemed like we got the first 80 percent of the song written fairly quickly but then we stalled on the last verse. Or, should I say, I stalled. Over those next few months I wrote 50 or more last verses to this song, and alas, none of them worked. "You have written a beautiful first 80 percent, Dennis," he said. "You have the listener in a trance. You want to *keep* them in a trance. Don't write a single word to take them out of that trance. "

I tried so hard and after many, many versions of the final verse, I wound up one day at my songwriter friend's farm outside of Nashville. After a glass or two of sweet tea and a barbeque lunch, he invited me into his writing room and asked me to play the current last verse to see if it was trance-worthy.

It was not. Heaving a sigh of frustration, I asked him if he ever wrote songs like that with so many versions of verses and choruses, etc. He didn't say a single word. He simply reached under his writing table and produced a 1-inch thick stack of yellow legal paper, all covered in handwritten words and scribbles and lines, and then he calmly slid it across the table to me with this single comment: "That, my friend....is *one song.*"

> He didn't say a single word. He simply reached under his writing table and produced a 1-inch thick stack of yellow legal paper, all covered in handwritten words and scribbles and lines, and then he calmly slid it across the table to me with this single comment: "That, my friend....is *one song.*"

Suddenly, it began to dawn on me why we only occasionally see greatness. It's a lot of work, and most people stop long before they have something exceptional. The people we revere, those who create those unforgettable standards in any field, are the ones who have taken the time to try and try again and are never satisfied until they have just *the* right word. And, that may take several legal pads and a box or two of pens to accomplish, metaphorically speaking.

I understand why people stop along the way, because after literally months of effort, I was exhausted with the song and tired of looking at it and singing it everywhere, including in my dreams, in my car, in the shower, and....

One night, right when I was dangling at or very near the end of my rope, my friend called me, and I asked him (pleaded, actually)... do you have any idea what this last verse should be? And, his answer made my heart leap.

He said, "How about this for the last verse?" And, then, he proceeded to produce the perfect last verse for this song. And, that's the beauty of having a capable co-writer. He or she can do things you cannot. And vice versa. But you have to stay humble, and you have to be willing to take direction.

> How often have you settled for *good* when *great* was possible?

Even if you decide not to use it, you still need the input because it's valuable and it's different than what you would have chosen.

Someone has well said that no writing is wasted. This may be surprising for some of you to hear, but you don't know everything, and two heads really are better than one. I guarantee it. But, take note—everybody shouldn't be your co-writer. You may have to work with a few before you find the one or two that you work best with. But, when you do, you can create some magic, something truly great.

So, what is *your* song? What one thing are you trying to communicate that really matters when you sit down to write?

How often have you settled for *good* when *great* was possible?

# How You
# Can Make Magic

I hope this book has been encouraging and helpful. That's really the reason I wrote it, after all.

So let me leave you with some simple ideas about how you can make magic happen with words.

# 1. Find a Co-writer/Editor

You've read it several times in this book, but I think it's important enough to say just one more time before we're done here.

This is really important. And, quite honestly, it may be the most difficult of all my recommendations, and here's why. You pour your heart and soul into something—anything—and then you go and hand it to someone else, basically to have them do a critique.

I have to tell you that, even after all these years of having editors and co-writers critique my work, the process still stings just a little. In fact, when I am finished writing this book, I am going to let a few very close and very trusted friends and advisors read it and give me their thoughts. Truthfully, I am *not* looking forward to their comments, even though I have asked for them.

This is my baby. I'm asking others if she's beautiful and smart or not. What I really want to hear is that this whole thing is nothing but sheer brilliance!

Why, it could be a classic!

Pure genius!

But, as we say here in Texas, you and I know that just ain't so. I make mistakes. I have probably left out something that really needs to be addressed here. I could have made a grammatical error, or misspelled a word or two. I may have droned on and on about something that should only be a paragraph or two at most. And, if I don't ask, no one is going to volunteer their opinion, and this book will not be as good as it could be.

That would sting a lot more than a little criticism.

## Senior Staff Writer

When I became a senior staff writer at The Gallup Organization, it was a rare privilege, and the first project they gave me in this new role made me very, very nervous. It's a little like standing in the gallery at The U.S. Open, and having one of the marshals walk over to the ropes and say, "I know you have always thought you could golf with the big boys, and we've all heard you talk big to your friends here about club selection and so forth, so today we're going to give you the privilege of seeing firsthand how you'd do. Come along with me, and I'll take you on over to the first tee. You'll need a collared shirt, and you'll have to pick a caddy from the caddy pool on site here.

"You'll be teeing off with Mr. Woods and Mr. Mickelson at 12:08. Oh, and just for fun, 50,000 people will be crammed around the first tee to see how you do, and they'll likely be commenting out loud on every shot you hit all day."

That's kind of what happened to me a decade or so ago. I had always written as an avocation. I had even had those aforementioned short articles published in *The Houston Chronicle* Sunday edition.

But suddenly, I got called out of the "gallery" one day at the storied Gallup Organization, and I was so rattled at first that I could hardly "swing the club." Before I knew it, I was on a plane headed down to Florida to interview the senior leadership of one of our client companies, and I was a wreck. I took a little tape recorder into each interview, wrote out a few questions that I thought might be pertinent, asked them (nervously, but with as much confidence as I could muster), took copious notes, and came home with a ton of information and quotes. My word limit for this piece was to be 1,800 or less, and my first draft of the article was almost 3,000 words.

But here's the point of this story. I sent that truckload of words off to Geoff Brewer, my editor, and he turned it into a succinct, beautiful, amazing, article that ran in *The Gallup Management Journal.* It was so well-received that a little later on, Gallup's CMO at the time stood up in a room filled with Gallup associates and announced that I was one of the top five writers in the Gallup Organization. I was stunned by that comment, and I'm not sure I believe it, but I have to tell you that none of it would have happened without my "co-writer," Geoff Brewer.

Yes, I thought those first 3,000 words were pretty good. But it wasn't hard to see that Geoff turned those 3,000 words into 1,800 brilliant ones that hung together beautifully and made so much more sense than what I could have accomplished alone.

So, figure out if you have associates or friends who understand you and your way of communicating. There's a lot of give-and-take in the process and it's important that this person also be someone who you trust implicitly, or who you can learn to trust. Their only agenda should be getting something great written, period.

## 2. Don't rush unless you have to

Look, I know everybody is in a hurry. Hardly anybody sits down to write anything for fun. You probably have a reason why you need to communicate more clearly and more effectively. And, you probably have a deadline. You're not doing this for your health.

We live in a fast-paced, get-it-done-yesterday environment, and the biggest danger we face is speeding along and just getting stuff done so we can mark it off our list.

Huge mistake.

Take your time. Think through your message. Plan out your writing time, if you can, to allow for some breathing room. Write it down, and then go back later and re-read it with fresh eyes. Check the taxonomy and the tone. I heard someone say once that it's hard to read the label when you're inside the bottle. That happens a lot. You're an expert and you use those terms every day in your work and life. But, are you writing to the uninitiated or someone who's never heard of this stuff (but should)?

We all have blind spots as writers. Take the time to let someone else look it over if you can.

Eventually, you'll get better at this. To continue the golf analogy, I can break 90 now pretty consistently. But, when I need real help, I go see a professional. Which brings me to tip # 3:

# 3. Hire a Pro

Okay. Maybe I'm supposed to be a little biased about this one, but it's true. I've spent many years doing this kind of work and there is something un-teachable after a point about doing really great writing.

Basically, I am my clients' co-writer, and I love it. They send me their rough drafts and it's easy for me to quickly see the issues that need to be addressed. In a way, I have become "Geoff Brewer' to my clients, and we have turned out some pretty nice work together over the years.

My clients seems to get the best results with some combination of #1 and #3. It seems like our best articles start with me writing a rough draft. Often, they will let an associate take a crack at the first edits. Then they send that version to me to make it final.

If I am working with a terrific writer, the process gets infinitely simpler. And, I try to teach my clients about what I am doing and why as we go through the process, so that at some point they can do really nice work without me.

# 4. Remember the three most important questions your audience is asking

- What's the message?
- Who's the messenger?
- Why should I care about it today?

Answer these correctly and doors will open and conversations that you need to happen will start.

# Epilogue

It's funny, isn't it, the twists and turns that life takes. When Mrs. McRee and I were standing in the library that September day all those years ago, I certainly couldn't have known where that newfound talent for words would lead me. I just wanted her to hurry up and finish talking so I could dive into that library of books.

But, in a way I was about to dive into a whole lot more. Over the next half century, communication and how it would be delivered would change exponentially. I have learned that even though technology has hastened the process of communication, people have not fundamentally changed. We still want to be touched and moved by the things we read and the movies and shows we see, and the songs we hear on our radios, iPods, or phones.

Most importantly I've learned that most everyone can accomplish the seemingly simple task of connecting with the person on the other end of the line and starting a conversation that matters.

I'm more than 50 years removed from that day in the library with Mrs. McRee, but I still love words just as much today, maybe even more. And part of the reason that love affair has grown is because I have seen firsthand what the right words, carefully chosen can do.

They're still magic.

So, make some magic of your own. Go out and change the world a little. Make people care about what you care about. And, when you do, please let me know about it by contacting me at Dennis@BeArticulate.com.

I never get tired of hearing a good story.

# a Book's Mind

Whether you want to purchase bulk copies of
*"So...what are you saying?"*
or buy another book for a friend, get it now at:
**www.BeArticulate.com**


**If you have a book that you would like to publish**,
contact A Book's Mind: info@abooksmind.com.


www.abooksmind.com

www.ingramcontent.com/pod-product-compliance
Lightning Source LLC
Chambersburg PA
CBHW051316220526
45468CB00004B/1368